The Happy Chef
Cannabis Cookbook

The Happy Chef
Cannabis Cookbook
By Deliciously Dee

Album **"The Prescription"**
By B- Real of Cypress Hill

Don't forget your **FREE** *music download!*

Deliciously Dee ™

CONTACT :
Danielle Russell,
M.C.C. Consulting in MMJ Production
dee@gbsciences.com
Bookings/Signings/Appearances
dee@deliciouslydee.com

Dedication

I want to dedicate this cannabis cookbook to my loving family. My sister Amber, who lost her life due to a prescription drug overdose February 2009. - & to my beautiful nephew, she gave me, Christopher aka the strongest man I know.

My loving father and mother, Joe and Karen. I have the most supportive parents a woman could ever hope for. My strength comes from the two that made me.

My brother Jason, his beautiful partner Julie and the blessing growing inside her at this very moment.

My beautiful happy best friend, The Happy Cat!

My amazing friends who are my family. I love you all! To my partners GBSciences for sharing my vision of combining science and art while formulating personalized medicine.

This cookbook was created as an alternative to smoking so that patients can adequately medicate. To all cannabis activists, employees, cultivators, scientists, botanists, geneticists, extractors, doctors, edible makers, artists, celebrities, and happy consumers who are pioneering the movement to legalize a very magical healing herb -

You ALL make me HAPPY!

Foreword by: Dr. Andrea Small-Howard

"Real World Cannabis Dosing and Infusions!" Chef Dee (aka. Deliciously Dee) is a consummate professional and her ten years of experience in the medical cannabis industry drives her passion to empower cannabis patients and cannabis lovers to make their own medicines and infused products based on sound culinary and scientific principles. Deliciously Dee provides scientifically-accurate, yet "real world" advise for dosing and infusing her delicious recipes, which are appropriate for both novice cannabis consumers, as well as canna-connoisseurs!

As a cannabis scientist for more than fifteen years, I trust Chef Dee's scientifically-informed approach to cannabis-infusions. I have even recommended her low dose edible formulations to patients who needed the kind of relief that these products provide.

Her accuracy and attention to detail may not be the first things that you notice if you have a chance to meet the vibrant and energetic Chef Dee in person, but it may be the reason that you keep coming back for sound advice on how to infuse with cannabis.

Dr. Andrea Small-Howard, Chief Science Officer of GB Sciences, Inc. (OTCQB: GBLX), has over 15 years experience studying cannabinoids and the endocannabinoid system, immunology and cancer treatments; as well as executive experience in the biopharmaceutical industry where she super vised research and development, manufacturing and quality control divisions.

In her biopharmaceutical career, Dr. Small-Howard took the lead in obtaining regulatory approvals from the U.S.

Food & Drug Administration ("US FDA") and multiple international regulatory agencies, and she has recently assisted state jurisdictions in developing medical cannabis regulations.

Dr. Small-Howard brings to GB Sciences a passion for advancing clinical research on medicinal applications of cannabinoid compounds in cannabis plants, clinical experience in conducting cannabinoid research, strategic vision for creating a vertically-integrated biopharmaceutical pipeline and a track record of successes in the management of biopharmaceutical companies. At GB Sciences, Dr. Small-Howard has been the co-inventor on two patents describing novel cannabis-based formulations for the treatment of neurological disorders (Parkinson's disease, Huntington's disease, dementia) and inflammatory disorders (arthritis, allergy, asthma, IBD, Crohn's disease). GB Sciences is committed to bringing novel cannabis-based therapies for life threatening medical conditions to the patients who need them.

Andrea L. Small-Howard, PhD, MBA Chief Science Officer & Director GB Sciences, Inc. (OTCQB:GBLX)

A Note from Deliciously Dee :

I hope you enjoy my recipes. My goal is to add to your quality of life, educate you and share how to cook with my favorite ingredient properly. If you enjoyed this cookbook, please gift it to a friend and help spread awareness. #CannabisIsMedicine

Introduction

Had a bad edible cannabis experience? Eat too much or not enough - trouble dosing? Or - perhaps you enjoy cooking with the plant or have an interest in joining the cannabis industry as a Canna Chef in an MMJ Production Lab. In either case - this is the book you need!

Whether you are new or an experienced medical marijuana patient, you probably have questions about the proper administration and dosing to create the desired therapeutic effects of cannabis products, safely.

"Deliciously Dee's - The Happy Chef expert cannabis cookbook" is the FIRST cannabis cookbook of its kind, giving the ultimate breakdown of the proper administration, extraction, and infusion of the cannabis plant to properly maximize the medicinal compounds and to medicate oneself to the desired level.

Thank you for purchasing Deliciously Dee's - The Happy Chef cannabis cookbook Dr Green Thumb Edition. Before we get canna cookin', let us get familiar with our main ingredient - The Herb.

(Photo By : Kayley Thomas-Garrett @kayleydaily)

I

The Herb

This chapter is a "crash course" in the understanding of the cannabis plant, its medical compounds and how it works in our bodies.

HOW DOES CANNABIS WORK?

In the mid-1960s, the science of marijuana began with the identification of delta-9-tetrahydrocannabinol (THC) as the main active ingredient in marijuana. Twenty years later, scientists identified the sites in the brain and body where marijuana acts and called them cannabinoid receptors - CB1 and CB2. Another discovery, which also acts on these CB receptors, was neurotransmitters-natural chemical messengers in our bodies called anandamide and 2-AG (2-arachidonoyl glycerol) which make up the endocannabinoid system (EC system).

The endocannabinoid system (EC system) is found in many areas of the brain, which explains why it affects so many different bodily functions. Cannabinoids exert their influence by regulating how cells communicate or how they send, receive and process messages. Anandamide then activates the cannabinoid receptors. Anandamide is a cannabinoid, like THC, but is a cannabinoid that your body already produces. THC will mimic the actions of anandamide, meaning that the THC binds with cannabinoid receptors and activates neurons, which causes euphoric effects on the mind and body and has been labeled over the years as the marijuana "high."

This "high" happens when high concentrations of cannabinoid receptors exist in the cerebellum, hippocampus and the basal ganglia of our brains causing pain relief in the consumer as well as other documented medicinal benefits. Those concentrations are now being studied for use in the treatment of many known patient ailments.

(Photo By : Master Cultivator Michelle of RadReeferCompany.com)

Many different strains possess different potency levels of therapeutic compounds, allowing each strain to be specified in the treatment of various patient ailments. Today - scientists, botanists, and geneticists are researching the variance in strains classifying each strain specification as a "personalized medicine" and is believed to be the future of cannabis as medicine. Scientists think, selectively bred cannabis plants can yield potent, high-performance medical marijuana containing over 480 natural components, including over 100 cannabinoids and 200 terpenoids.

The plant contains buds, or flowers, covered in a sticky dusting of crystal resin, which contains hundreds of therapeutic compounds known as cannabinoids and terpenoids.cannabis strains can vary widely in the quantity of cannabinoids and terpenoids that they produce, which is apparent in differences in color, smell, and taste. These medical compounds can effect the body differently, which makes having basic understanding of their effects critical to patient care.

Cannabinoids are a class of diverse chemical compounds that act on cannabinoid receptors in cells that alter neurotransmitter releases in the brain, found in all living beings except insects. The cannabis plant produces more than 100 phyto-cannabinoids or cannabinoids that are naturally occurring within the cannabis family.

Most common cannabinoids:
- tetrahydrocannabiarian (THCV)
- delta-8-tetrahydrocannabinol (delta-8-THC)
- delta-9-tetrahydrocannabinol (THC)
- cannabidiols (CBD)
- cannabigerols (CBG)
- cannabinol (CBN)
- cannabichromenes (CBC)
- cannabindiol (CBDL)
- canabicyclol (CBL)
- cannabielsoin (CBE)
- cannabitriol (CBT)
- There are many other phyto-cannabinoids that exist in trace amounts and have not yet been thoroughly investigated.

The differences between cannabinoids are determined by the extent to which they are psychologically active.

The well known THC has psychoactive effects, as does CBN and CBDL, three classes of cannabinoids- the CBG, CBC and CBD are not known to have such an effects. There

19

receptors. Anandamide, nicknamed "the bliss molecule.", comes from the San skrit word for "joy, bliss, or happiness" and plays a role in pain relief, appetite, memory, depression and fertility and may lead to the development of an entirely new family of therapeutic medicine.

Terpenoids are the essential oils of the cannabis plant. The unique smell of cannabis arises from the over 100 terpenoid compounds, not from cannabinoids. These compounds are a large and diverse class of organic compounds produced by a variety of plants and also some insects, such as swallowtail butterflies. These compounds are easily extracted from the cannabis plant material by steam distillation. Various plant terpenoids possess antibacterial, and herbal remedies that can remediate the effects of THC.

Most common terpenoids:
- alfa and beta pinene
- alfa-terpineol
- borneol
- terpineol-4-ol
- linalool
- d-limonene
- 1.8-cineole (eucalyptol)
- delta-3-carene
- beta-myrcene
- beta-caryophyllene

Plant terpenoids are used for their aromatic qualities and also play a role in traditional herbal remedies. One terpenoid found in the cannabis plant, d-lim onene, can also be found in a lemon peel. In fact, terpenoids contribute to the scent of eucalyptus and lavender, the flavors of cinnamon, chocolate, cloves and ginger, the yellow color in sun flowers and also the color red in tomatoes. Also, vitamin A found in beer, is a terpenoid. The aroma and flavor of hops comes from terpenes, alpha-humulene, be ta-caryophyllene, and sesquiterpenes, which have an affect on thebeers quality.

Flavonoids are widely distributed in plants and fulfill many functions. They are the most important plant pigments for flower coloration, producing yellow or red/blue pigmentation in petals designed to attract pollinator animals. They may also act as chemical messengers, cell cycle inhibitors, and physiological regulators. The cannabis plant produces up to 20 different known flavonoids.

Most common flavonoids:
- quercetin
- cannaflavin A
- apienin
- beta-sitosterol

(Photo By : Master Cultivator Michelle of RadReeferCompany.com)

Photo By : Master Cultivator Michelle of RadReeferCompany.com

Flavonoids are aromatic, polycyclic compounds that induce known pharmacological activity as well. The pharmacokinetics of THC are modulated by flavonoids via the inhibition of P450 enzymes, which shield healthy cells from pro-carcinogens such as benzo-a-pyrene and aflatoxins, potentially found in cannabis smoke from being activated into carcinogens. Specific flavonoids, such as apigenin, inhibit the production of tumor necrosis factor-alpha (TNF-a) that maintains and induces inflammation. Apigenin is also known to be a strong anxiolytic agent without the side effects of synthetic benzodiazepines such as sedation.

Cannabis Entourage Effect

The interactive and therapeutic synergies of various compounds in marijuana is what scientists refer to as the "cannabis entourage effect." The "entourage effect", also called the "therapeutic ensemble", was a phrase introduced in cannabinoid science in 1998 by S. Ben-Shabat with Raphael Mechoulam to represent the various amounts of isolated or combined cannabinoids and terpenoids useful in the treatment of a wide range of patient conditions. It's defined as the broad-spectrum sense of wellness derived from consuming concentrated or an unaltered form of cannabis.

Any single chemical in isolation does not perform in the same way that a substance will when associated with other

er chemicals found in the original, natural source. The three primary components of the marijuana chemical cocktail include CBD, THC and the phyto-cannabinoid group of terpenoids. CBD by itself performs differently than CBD in conjunction with THC, and both perform differently when in the presence of terpenoids. Marijuana's effect and strength varies by strain based on the ratio of these three components. All the natural chemicals found in cannabis are ingested simultaneously utilizing the full spectrum of therapeutic compounds cannabis has to offer. This modern approach in the medicinal use of cannabis leverages the full potential of this chemical synthesis rather than reducing the naturally occurring pharmacology to a single component, which is known as **"whole plant medicine."**

Researchers have discovered that THC and other cannabinoid and terpenoid agents can be combined to produce therapeutic synergies that offer relief in the following:

Category	Symptom	Medical Value	Cannabinoid & Terpenoids
Bone Disorder	Degenerative bone diseases	Bone Growth Stimulant	CBC, CBD, CBDV, CBG, THCV
Cancer	Malignant tumors	Anti-proliferative	CBC, CBD, CBDA, CBG, delta—THC, THCA, beta-caryophyllene, beta-Myrcene, Cineol, Citronellol, alpha-humulene, Limonene
	Defense	Antioxidant	
Circulatory	Ischemia	Anti-ischemic	CBD, Caryophyllene oxide, Cineol
	Poor Blood Circulation	Vaso-relaxant	CBC
Diabetes	Diabetes	Anti-Diabetic	CBD
Eating Disorders	Acid Reflux	Anti-Prokinetic	CBD, CBDA
	Ulcers	Gastoroprotective	Cineol
	Constipation	Laxative	Guaiol
	Nausea	Anthiemetic	CBD, Delta-8-THC Isopulegol
	No Appetite, Wasting	Appetite Stimulator	Delta-8-THC, Delta- -THC
	Obesity, Weight management	Anorectic) Appetite suppressant)	THCV, Alpha-Humulene
Ocular Disease	Glaucoma	Eye pressure reducer	Delta- THC

Category	Symptom	Medical Value	Cannabinoid & Terpenoids
Infections	Bacterial Infection	Anti-Bacterial, Antiseptic	CBC, CBD, CBG, CBN, delta— THC, alpha-bisabolol, Borneol, alpha-pinene, beta-caryophyllene, beta-pinene, Camphene, Cineol, Limonene, Linalool, Terpinolene
	Fungal Infection	Anti-fungal	
	Microbial Infection	Anti-microbial	
	Viral Infection	Anti-Viral	
			CBC, CBG, alpha- Pinene, Beta-Caryophyllene, beta-Eudesmol, caryophyllen oxide, cineol, limonene, linalool, nerolidol, terpinolene
			CBD, apha-Terpinene, Citronellol, Linalool
			Limonene, Linalool
Joint Disorders	Lupus Rheumatoid arthritis	Immunosuppressive	CBD
Liver Disease	Hepatotoxicity	Antihepatotoxic	beta-Eudesmol, Cineol
Mental Health & Well-Being	Anxiety	Anxiolytic	CBD, Delta-8-THC, Limonene, Linalool
	Depression	Sedative	Cineol, gamma-Terpinene, Limonene, Linlool
	Psychosis	Antidepressants	
	Neurodegenerative Diseases	Antipsychotic	CBD, delta-8-THC
		Neuroprotective	CBD. delta-8-THC, delta--THC
	Seizure Disorders	Anti-Convulsive	CBD, CBDV, CBN, THCV, Linalool
Muscle Disorders	Spasms	Anti-Spasmodic	CBD, CBN, delta-8-THC, delta- -THC, THCa, beta-Myrcene, Clneol, Citronellol, Isopulegol, Limonene, Linalool
Organ Transplant Care	Minimize Rejection	Allograft Stimulant	CBD
Pain	Pain	Analgesic	CBC, CBD, CBG, CBGA, CBN, delta-8- THC, delta-THC, beta-Myrcene, Borneol, Isopulegol
	Pain	Anesthetic	Cineol, Linalool
	Inflamation	Anti-Inflammatory	CBC, CBD, CBG, CBGA, CBGVA, CBN, CBNA, delta- -THC, THCA, aplpha-bisabolol, alpha-Humulene, alpha-Pinene, beta-Caryophyllene, beta-Myrcene, Cineol,

Category	Symptom	Medical Value	Cannabinoid & Terpenoids
			Citronellol, delta-3-Carane, limonene, Linalool, Ocimene
Respiratory	Allergic asthma COPD ——————— Congestion ——————— Congestion	Bronchodilator Broncho-relaxant ————————— Decongestant ————————— Expectorant	Delta- -THC, aplha-Pinene, Borneol, Cineol, Limonene, Linalool —————— Camphene, Cineol, Isopulegol, Limonene —————— Cineol, Camphene, Limonene, Linalool
Skin Disorders	Itching Psoriasis	Anti-psoriatic Antipruritic	CBD Caryophyllene oxide, Cineol
Sleep Disorders	Fatigue ———— Insomnia ———— Sleep apnea	Anti-fatigue ———— Sleep Aid ———— Sleep apnea easer	Cineol —————— CBC, CBD, CBN, beta-Myrcene, Borneol, Citronellol, Linalool, Nerolidol, Phytol, Terpinolene —————— delta- -THC

(Photo By Kayley Garrett)

25

(Photo By : Shawn Gower @waxpuddle)

II

Forms of Medical Cannabis

Today, medical marijuana-based products can be purchased by cannabis patients in a variety of forms. This is good news for the medical marijuana patient, as it allows customization of patient treatment with the use of different cannabis compounds to facilitate therapeutic goals. It can also present a challenge. Too many choices can confuse or overwhelm patients, especially those new to cannabis. So, to clear up any confusion, this chapter outlines and breaks down the most common forms of medical cannabis.

CONCENTRATES

Concentrates is the term used in reference to any product derived through a cannabinoid extraction process. Cannabinoids and terpenoids are isolated by extraction, either by physical means or with the use of fats, oils, alcohol or solvents to make cannabis concentrates. Kosher vegetable glycerin is another effective way for extracting cannabis to make concentrates directly from the plant material. Vegetable-based glycerin is innocuous and used in many products, including cough syrups. Many concentrates are abundant in specific cannabinoids, such as delta-9-tetrahydrocannabinol (THC) or cannabidiol (CBD). Known for its psychoactive and pain-killing effects, THC is the most popular cannabinoid, while CBD offers the most health benefits without the "high" effects on your mood and perception. Cannabis concentrates are available in an increasing number of forms, such as cannabis oil, hashish, salve, and tinctures.

CRYSTALS (CBD, THC)

Crystals are extracted down to a powder, crystal form of the plant, are considered the highest quality, from seed to finished product with also reaching the highest potency levels ranging in the 90 percentile. The process of formulating crystals safe starts with the extraction process, followed by winterization to remove the fats and lipids. Unwanted

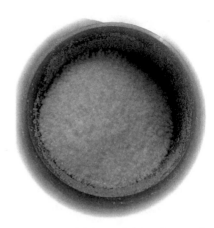

(Photo: CBD Crystals lab tested at 99.9% potency)

plant material is then removed with a rotary evaporator. The oil then goes through a secondary rotary evaporation process and is decarboxylated prior to going into the final phase of creating CBD, THC crystals. The result of these established phytoceutical and pharmaceutical refinement and distillation methods is 99%+ pure CBD,THC isolate for consumer and manufacturing needs.Crystals work well in the emulsification process or when being infused into foods, liquids, nutritional supplements, topicals, and even cosmetics.

EDIBLES

Edibles are available in a variety of forms that range from brownies, lozenges, gummies, and granola bars to beverages such as coffees and teas infused with cannabis extracts. Producers of edibles often make their own extract by slow-cooking cannabis plant material in a fat, such as a oil or butter. As you'll learn in Chapter 4, Deliciously Dee's preferred infusion techniques in such food consistencies that maximize the medicinal benefits from each compound found in cannabis. Cannabis oil, hash ish and hashish oil can also be

28

dissolved into milk and consumed in drinks, milk being the carrier of choice due to its empulsive properties as cannabis is an oil-based substance. Edibles, when made by an amateur can be dangerous. Although consuming too much isn't fatal,

(Photo By Kayley Garrett:Relax With Happy Strawberry Shortie Cakebites)

the effects can be most unpleasant: vomiting, dizziness, inability to talk, inability to walk - not enjoyable effects to be had by anyone. When consumed, with the proper knowledge of the cannabis plant you are working with, to learning the basic formulas laid out in this cook book, you will have no problem reaching your desired level of medication.

Deliciously Dee ™ recommended doses for different tolerance levels is recommended in Chapter 3: Dee-carb. *When in doubt of any cannabis-infused product, please DO NOT consume that product.

Make sure to look for Relax With Happy ™ edibles in your local dispensary. Lab tested at state certified, Digi-Path Labs.

(Photo By Kayley Garrett:Relax With Happy Medi Chew. Phunky Feel Tip)

FLOWERS

Flower is an unprocessed form of marijuana, consisting of the leaves and buds of the female Cannabis Sativa and Cannabis Indica plants. Cannabis flowers, also known as buds, are removed from harvested plants, carefully dried and cured, tested for potency and safety by a state accredited laboratory, packaged, and sold by weight using a seed to sale tracking system , such as Metrc, BioTrackTHC or MJ Freeway. I recommend purchasing your cannabis flowers at a local dispensary as all products sold are tested for potency, microbial, solvents and pesticides guaranteeing good quality, consistent and clean medicine.

HASHISH

Hashish, or hash for short, is a preparation of marijuana made from the resin of the Cannabis Sativa or Cannabis Indica plant. For thousands of years hashish has been produced using heat and force to mechanically compress kief an varying amounts of cannabis flowers and leaf fragments into blocks. It can be solid or resinous, depending on how it's produced. It is named by the way it reacts to heat, as shown below:

Name	Consistency
Bubble	Initially Bubbles
Full Bubble	Bubbles throughout the entire heating process
Melt	Melts or turns into sticky Oil
Full Melt	Fully melts and leaves little to no residue

There are several different types of hashish, and their colors range from dark brown or almost black, through various shades of brown, to a dirty yellowish color. The appearance of different types of hashish can vary from looking dark and shiny, a bit like licorice, to being lighter and dull or matte, a bit like a stock cube. The texture of hashish also varies from quite dry and hard, like piece of fudge, to moist and pliable.

HASH OIL

Hash oil is made by employing solvent or non-solvent extraction methods, is one of the strongest forms of marijuana, and is the least common form of the plant. The oil is a tacky liquid that retains a robust terpenoid-rich flavor profile and moderate THC levels. It is sold in plastic syringes, tiny bottles or sealed plastic bags and only a small amount is needed to produce the effects of marijuana. Typically, marijuana hash oil is smoked in a pipe, painted onto cigarettes - joints, or used in making edibles.

KIEF

Also known as "pollen" or "dry sift", is the bulbous crystal formation on the tip of a gland that contains a high concentration of terpenoids and cannabinoids. Kief can be eaten raw, smoked, vaporized, or is used to make hashish and edibles.

SUPPOSITORIES

Administered rectally, cannabis suppositories are usually about an inch in length and made with either cannabis-infused coconut oil or a mixture of solid propane hash oil and coconut oil. This form of medicating is designed to melt in the body. Store in refrigerator to keep solid until needed.

TINCTURES

Tinctures are herbal extracts usually made using glycerin or alcohol. Cannabis tinctures are most effectively administered sub-lingually, under the tongue, but they can be added to food and beverages and are sometimes flavored to improve their taste.

Tinctures are liquid concentrates generally pro cured using alcohol to extract the cannabinoids from the cannabis plant. Cannabis alcohol tinctures were the primary format of marijuana-based medications prior to the cannabis ban of 1937. These tinctures come in small jars with droppers in the lid. Just a few drops. drops under your tongue and you will begin to feel the effects, relatively quickly. Transcend Hemp. Enhanced Products Cannabis tinctures are inexpensive and easy to make compared to other concentrates and are the preferred method of consumption by many patients.

TOPICALS

Topically administered cannabis-infused products include creams, salves, lotions and even personal lubricant and are typically made with alcohol or slowly heating cannabis in olive oil, coconut oil, or beeswax to extract the cannabinoids and terpenoids. Cannabis topicals treat typical athletic aches and pains by leveraging the physiology behind the endocannabinoid system.

GI Issues : Cannabis is known to relieve pain, calm peristaltic spasms, and regulate motility.

(Photo By Kayley Garrett)

Joint & Muscle Pain : Cannabis lotions, oils and salves, applied to a localized area, absorb into affected muscles and joints, reducing inflammation and pain directly where it occurs.

Sexual stimulant: Cannabis-infused personal lubricant adds buzzy, tingly sensations when applied to the clitoris or tip of the penis. Medicated lubricant is normally a coconut oil based product. As the vagina is a mucous membrane, the medicine is absorbed quickly - stimulating the area where applied. The powerful effects are normally felt during foreplay.

Skin irritation : Cannabis has natural anti-fungal, anti-bacterial, anti-viral and anti-inflammatory properties. It reduces pain, swelling and possible infection from chafing, mild rashes, psoriasis and acne. Also known to speed healing and provide pain relief from sunburn.

Cannabis-infused topicals are also formulated as transdermal patches which are then applied to the skin to deliver medication locally and over a period of time.

WAX

Marijuana wax, is a cannabis concentrate, also called "earwax," because of its color, or just "wax", that contains high levels of THC. It is also called "earwax," because of its color, or just "wax", that contains high levels of THC. It is also called BHO, which is an abbreviation of "butane hash oil" or "butane honey oil" which name derives from the color and the solvent used in the extraction process.

(Photo:TapRoot Vape Extracts)

Waxes are extracted from flowers using a solvent, most commonly carbon dioxide, oxygen, or butane. After the extraction process, the solvent is purged using cold or heat evaporation methods. The solvents used in this process can leave behind toxic residues. Testing labs carefully screen waxes to ensure safety.

Wax names refer to their consistency :

Name	Consistency
Budder	Creamy, like paste. Retains many terpenes, and possess THC levels over 70%
Honeycomb, Crumble	Dry and crumbly texture. Perforated with holes like a honeycomb
Shatter, Glass	Smooth, translucent, and firm like a hard candy- A second extraction process that removes fats, lipids, and waxes make it extremely potent- over 80% THC but- this process destroys most terpenoids.
Taffy	Firmer than sap, but not brittle like shatter

(Photo: Crumble)

(Photo: Shatter)

Waxes are typically vaporized or burned - "dabbed." The term "dabbing" is a popular method of administering cannabis wax products amongst many in the cannabis community. These potent waxes are also used in cooking edibles, topicals, and were the inspiration to the oh so popular - Relax With Happy ™ EDIBLE SLABS.

(Photo By Kayley Garrett)

III

Administering Cannabis

For the past century, medical marijuana has had a rocky history. With the new discoveries and ongoing research on the cannabis plant, more and more people are becoming comfortable with it. Each year, more and more states have been legalizing marijuana for medicinal use as well as recreational or adult-use.

As you learned in the previous section, cannabis is available in a number of forms. So, let us now dive into the different administration methods of cannabis so that you may find your preferred method of consumption. Cannabis can be administered in a variety of ways and the method depends on the medicinal effects desired by the patient. Some methods offer prolonged relief affecting the entire body, some offer targeted relief to a localized area, while others are designed to provide fast relief. For instance, vaporizing or smoking cannabis can bring immediate relief as a bronchodilator to patients suffering from allergies or asthma. Athletes or those suffering from an injury may seek a more targeted relief, such as a topical or transdermal product, while patients who suffer from sleep disorders or chronic pain might benefit from the long lasting, whole-body analgesic effects gained from edibles.

Gaining the medical and physical benefits of cannabis is largely dependent upon how it's cultivated, produced and consumed. Each method provides a unique experience and host of effects. In this section we explore each method, dosing and medicinal affects so that the patient may better select their preferred method of administration. There are three basic delivery methods: ***oral, topical, and inhalation***. Under these umbrella methods are various techniques appropriate for different occasions and serve unique functions.

So for those aspiring to become a comprehensive cannabis aficionado, let this be your guide and experiment with the different methods of consuming cannabis - who knows – you could find a new favorite.

Oral Methods

EDIBLES

Edibles are one of the most well-known and also the most feared methods of administering cannabis medicine. These cannabinoid and terpenoid infused products are sold in many different forms, including cooking oils, health foods, desserts, beverages, candies, and even chewing gum and is a popular form of administering for patients who cannot tolerate, or wish to avoid smoking.

The major risk associated with administering edibles is accidental over intoxication, particularly among new medical cannabis patients. When edibles are digested and metabolized by our bodies, the THCA is processed in the liver into 11-hydroxy-THC, which is twice as strong and works twice as long as inhaled delta-9. Over intoxication can be avoided by my Deliciously Dee's™ recommended infusion methods and dosing procedures listed in Chapter 3: Dee-carb.

(Photo by Kayley Garrett: Relax With Happy- Medicinal Chews)

As everyone's metabolism is different, it could take between 30 minutes to several hours to feel the effect of the edible consumed. With this knowledge, please wait a sufficient length of time before consuming more as many users report effects peaking at two hours and lasting for about four to six hours. Experts recommend starting with a very small dose for those inexperienced with edibles to discover their bodies time clock in metabolizing ingestible cannabis products.

RAW CANNABIS

(Photo: Bubba Kush)

In the method of ingesting raw cannabis, compared to other methods of delivery, a large amount of cannabis may be required to achieve the desired therapeutic benefit. Freshly harvested cannabis, when eaten, is reported to reduce inflammation while minimizing psycho-activity.

SUBLINGUAL

When administering cannabis sublingually (under the tongue), the medicine is rapidly absorbed into the arterial system and quickly transported to the brain and other organs, offering fast relief for its patients. It is an excellent alternative to inhalation offered normally in the form of cannabis tinctures.

Reaching appropriate dosage amounts when administering tinctures are dependent upon many factors, including the potency of the tincture, the tolerance level of the patient, and meeting the patient's unique medical requirements. Dose control, or titration, is easily achieved by counting the number of drops administered under the tongue. Experts recommend starting with a few drops, waiting several minutes, then administering additional drops if necessary, and repeating until desired therapeutic outcome is achieved.

- Medicated gummies and hard candies are absorbed both sublingually and through the digestive tract, so the effects are different from a pure sublingual medication or edible.

SUPPOSITORIES

Suppositories are a solid dosage form that are inserted into the rectum where the medicinal compounds are quickly absorbed through the intestinal wall directly into the bloodstream. Patients that used cannabis suppositories reported the effects beginning to work 10-15 minutes after insertion into the rectum, and lasting between 4-8 hours. They are used to deliver both locally and systemically acting medications.

TEA

The potency of medical cannabis teas has a significant effect on the way cannabis is steeped. In activating the medical compounds in cannabis, the non-psychoactive compound THCA is converted to the medical and psychoactive compound THC as a result of the heat applied when smoking, vaporizing, or cooking the cannabis with butter or oils. This does not occur when steeping it to make tea because the temperature of the hot water does not get high enough to decarboxylate THCA, which requires temperatures above 246° degrees Fahrenheit.

In cannabis teas, as in all cannabis products, the cannabinoid and terpenoid levels are affected by each compound's solubility and decarboxylation factors. The preparation controls the amount of active cannabinoids and terpenoids in the tea. For a "mild" dose, steep dry flowers and leaves in hot water to begin to take the edge off your day. If desiring a "medium" dose, equivalent to one to four alcoholic beverages, steep a blend of cannabis infused with a fat, such as coconut oil or butter, in hot water to make a chai - or latte-style drink. You may also steep the mixture of cannabis in hot water containing a cannabis tincture, or added infused honey or milk.

Topical Methods

TOPICALS, TRANSDERMAL

The decision of which kind of topical a patient uses depends on the therapeutic goal. In topicals, isolated cannabinoids and terpenoids quickly absorb into the skin layers but do not have any psychoactive effects, making them ideal for athletes, those who drive a vehicle, and or operate heavy equipment.

These isolated components can be suspended in delivery mediums such as creams, lotions, ointments, balms, gels, salves, topical sprays, and transdermal patches.

Topicals offer localized treatment for patients who suffer from:
• Abrasions (both cutaneous and subcutaneous)
• Arthritis
• Joint pain
• Muscle pain
• Sports injuries
• Surgical pain

Transdermal patches contain isolated cannabinoids and terpenoids that can be applied to any area of the skin to deliver a localized, time-released dose of one or more isolated cannabinoids to a problematic area. Transdermal patches last longer than creams, but their effects do not kick in as quickly.

Inhalation Methods

When cannabis is inhaled, the gases enter the lungs before absorbing into the bloodstream. The potency is affected by many factors, such as strain and moisture levels, which are identified by an state certified testing laboratory and identified on the product packaging or by other information-access means, online with sample test results. There are currently three prevalent types of inhalation methods: dabbing, smoking, and vaping.

DABBING

Dabbing is one of the most popular methods for consuming marijuana concentrates. It often results in a very intense high, so it is rarely recommend, if ever, for new cannabis users. While not fatal, over intoxication on THC can result in nausea, dizziness, and loss of consciousness and is easy to do, especially to those who are new to this method.

Dabs are doses of cannabis concentrates containing THC levels approaching 90 percent, termed as either butane hash oil, shatter, or wax, which are heated to a high temperature, using a torch, and inhaled. This delivery method may be appropriate to treat chronic pain or extreme nausea. Dabbing burns concentrate at temp -eratures very close to THC's vaporization point -- making dabs one of the healthier smoking methods. Although there are obvious health benefits associated with clean concentrates over combustible flower, concerns arise from dabbing's image and the intense effects of high-THC extracts.

SMOKING

Cannabis is commonly smoked in hand-rolled cigarettes, known as "joints," "spliffs," or "doobies." The burn ing and inhaling of dried/cured cannabis flowers rolled in paper, or through a pipe or bong, delivers fast results as the medicinal compounds released move quickly through the airway, lungs, and bloodstream, where they become bio-available to the brain and other organs. Hashish and cannabis flower can be mixed with rolling tobacco (a soft, moist, sticky tobacco preparation designed for hand-rolling) or the dry tobacco from deconstructed cigarettes. The technique of warming then crumbling hashish into hand-rolled joints is an important part of the ritual of marijuana use in some circles, and a giveaway clue that you are with an experienced user.

Heavy users of marijuana in particular may own and use a variety of paraphernalia for marijuana consumption. Paraphernalia is the term used for the equipment used to inhale cannabis, hashish and hashish oil coming in the forms of "one hitters" or "dug-outs", pipes, water pipes, and or bongs. If you are in the company of people who use elaborate bongs or pipes, be aware - you are again in the presence of an experienced user.

Smoking imposes health dangers since cannabis contains many of the same dangerous combustible materials found in conventional tobacco cigarettes which is the drawback to this method of administration. Although, there have been studies suggesting that the compounds in cannabis mitigate many of the adverse health effects of the carcinogenic fumes produced by burning combustible materials.

*Many lose their lives to cigarettes. Please if you are a smoker -- QUIT NOW! It does nothing good for you and you're paying someone to kill yourself slowly. There are zero benefits to smoking cigarettes. Life is precious and so are you!

If you have to smoke, smoke cannabis -
NOT cigarettes!

VAPORIZING

Vaporizers are the logical choice for moderate to experienced and/or health-conscious cannabis consumers. Like smoking, vaporizing cannabis (often called "vaping") delivers fast results. In this method, instead of burning the plant material, a vaporizer steadily heats marijuana to a temperature of around 180°-200°   degrees celsius, or 356°-392° degrees Fahrenheit, that is high enough to extract THC, CBD, and other cannabinoids, but the temperatures are too low for the potentially harmful toxins that are released during combustion as is with smoking a joint. When inhaling raw flowers or buds , as is the same with tobacco, you are inhaling charred plant matter.

*MAPS and NORML conducted a feasible study that confirmed vaporizers could successfully generate cannabinoids at 185° degrees celsius while completely suppressing the formation of unhealthy substances such as naphthalene, benzene, and toluene - which are produced when cannabis and tobacco are smoked.

They are sold in a variety of shapes and sizes, ranging

8⊕%
THC

⊖
HYBRID

roots

(www.Taproot-holding.com)

from pocket-sized "vape pens" that run on batteries to large tabletop devices that plug into a wall and are a preference for many cannabis patients. Also has the known benefit of an equally significant reduction in odor, which is great for patients who prefer to be discreet. -

Pro Tip : A 500mg vape cartridge is normally consumed after 400 draws, at a rate of 0.3 mg of tetrahydrocannabinol (THC) per draw by the average patient.

WARNING

Medical marijuana must be administered as directed by and under the supervision of a qualified physician, who must first rule out potential interactions with other prescription, over-the-counter, and herbal medications. It is important to use cannabis products as directed on packaging and as recommended by your physician.

The consulting physician can create a treatment that specifies which cannabinoids and terpenoids are most likely to work in treating the patient's medical condition, so that the patient can work with the dispensary and/or cannabis testing laboratory to find the right cannabis products. The treatment plan should also include the amount of cannabis-based medication to administer, the dosage frequency, and acceptable methods of administering.

If located in Las Vegas Nevada, I recommend Valley Center for Cannabis Therapy to all of my patients. Contact them directly or request that your primary doctor contact on your behalf for a more expedited consultation.

CONVERSE WITH YOUR PHYSICIAN

Whether or not medical marijuana will be helpful to you can only be determined through close work with your health care provider.

Talking about cannabis can be intimidating and confusing, especially to new consumers, however - it is important to ask "the right" questions so one may get the treatment they need. It is always best to do your own research before you meet with your healthcare provider. A little research will make you more comfortable and better prepare you for your consultation.

Questions to ask your physician:
- Does medical cannabis seem like a good option for my ailment(s)?
- What types of ailments can be treated with medicinal marijuana?
- What is the best administering method of cannabis with my ailment? (vaporizers, edibles, suppositories, topicals, etc)
- Will I be able to preform my every day duties and lifestyle while using medical cannabis?
- Advice for safe consumption of medical marijuana?
- Will the prescribed medical marijuana interact with my other medications?

In addition to these questions, it is good to write down a few questions that are specific to your medical history.

The following list of illnesses are eligible for medical marijuana treatment and has been identified by the Nevada Division of Public Health (DBPH):

- Cancer
- Glaucoma
- HIV, AIDS

- Any medical condition producing cachexia (weakness and wasting), severe nausea, chronic pain, or persistent muscle spasms or seizures.

DOSAGES

The potency of the known cannabis compounds varies by strain, when and how the plant is harvested, and how it is processed. Each of these compounds at different potency levels have different effects on the body, making dosing complicated for a beginner cannabis consumer. Ongoing research proves cannabis compounds therapeutic significance in treating specific medical conditions. The treatment of these medical conditions, similar to prescription medications, comes weighed out in milligram doses for the consumer. I have listed Deliciously Dee's recommended doses in chapter 3: Dee-carb.

DRUG INTERACTIONS

Cannabis should not be used in combination with any medications that induce drowsiness or slow down the central nervous system. Such medications include muscle relaxants, sleeping pills, tranquilizers, pain killers, anti-seizure medications, and certain antihistamines and cold medicines. Discuss with your physician before using cannabis, its interactions with all prescription drugs, over-the-counter medicines, and herbal products you use as cannabis can interact with those drugs.

DRUG TESTING

THC can be detected in most drug tests and remain in your system for several weeks to months after cannabis use.

SIDE EFFECTS OF CANNABIS USE

Cannabis use may cause delusions, hallucinations, and amnesia, can alter your mood and cause you to experience strange sensations.

You may experience feelings of:

- agitation
- anxiety
- bloodshot eyes
- coughing
- dizziness
- dry mouth
- enhanced sensory perceptions
- euphoria
- facial flushing
- headache
- inability to concentrate
- loss of inhibitions
- paranoia
- relaxation
- time-distortion

These unpleasant feelings or side effects resolve in short time after stopping medical marijuana use.

Medical marijuana is NOT recommended for patients:

- Allergic to cannabis or compounds found in cannabis.
- Pregnant, planning to get pregnant, or nursing.
- Suffering from severe depression, or having a history of schizophrenia or other serious mental illness.

Patient Responsibilty

KNOWING YOUR MEDICINE

Talk to your healthcare provider to make sure you are using appropriate dosage that works for you. Your medications are for you and you only. Medical cannabis, like many other medications, has different effects on different people, so don't share it with friends, family members, or children. Make sure you're following your healthcare provider's recommendations and listening to dispensary employee feedback to ensure you are not overusing your medication.

STORING YOUR MEDICINE

It is important to properly store your cannabis medicine. In order to get the best results out of your medical marijuana, save it in an airtight container - as oxygen ages and drys out the plant. If you are buying dried marijuana, it is best kept out of direct sunlight. Edibles can look especially appealing to both pets and children, so make sure to avoid any mishaps by keeping edible products in a sealed airtight packaging in a locking security bag - keep in freezer for longer shelf life. Be conscious of and where you store all cannabis-infused products, making sure it is kept out of reach of children and pets at all times. Unless your children are medically authorized to use medical marijuana, it is illegal to dispense to your children. Basically, treat your medical marijuana as you treat other medications.

(Photo by Kayley Garrett: Relax With Happy- Medicinal Chews)

Deliciously Dee's preferred method of decarboxylation.

IV

Dee-Carb

DOSING

The problem with most unexperienced cannabis chefs is putting in too much of your medicine. In this chapter is a break down of decarboxylation, extraction and dosing properly to maximize the full potencies of your cannabis medicine. Decarboxylation is the process of converting the acidic forms of phytocannabinoids (such as CBDA or THCA) to the non-acidic or "activated" form (CBD or THC) by using heat to gently break the bond of the acid group.

Edibles, when purchased at a dispensary, normally come in milligram (mg) dosing provided with a lab test in purchased child-proof edible packaging.

The state standards for how to report a "dose" are well established as the edibles are generally weighed out per milligram dose of the net weight of the unit and are lab tested for potency, microbial, solvents, and pesticides. Another difference is in the concentration of the medicine(s) and/or portion(s) the patient consumes.

The consumption of cannabis medicine by inhaling the cannabis plant is different from consuming that of edibles. Edibles offer a healthy alternative to medicate rather than smoking, as you are not inhaling smoke there are no damages to your respiratory system which helps if you are unable to smoke or prefer not to. When cooking edibles there is risk that you may not have decarboxylated, cooked or heated, the cannabis long enough to extract the active ingredient. Those edibles will contain a different form of cannabinoids from those that are heated, either when consumed or in baking.

You have THCA and you have THC for example :

At most about 75% of the THCA molecules end up as THC (delta-9) molecules.
Please respect the decarboxylation process.

Ounces (oz)	Grams (g)	Millagrams (mg)
1 ounce	28 grams	28,000mg
1/2 ounce	14 grams`	14,000mg
1/8 ounce	3.5 grams	3,500mg
	1 gram	1000mg

So lets say for example your flower medicine only has a 10% total active medical components.

Ounces (oz)	Grams (g)	Millagrams (mg)	10% Total Active Cannabinoids
1 ounce	28 grams	28,000mg	2,800mg active
1/2 ounce	14 grams`	14,000mg	1,400mg active
1/8 ounce	3.5 grams	3,500mg	350mg active
	1 gram	1000mg	100mg active

The decarboxylation process starts around 220° Fahrenheit (104°C) and can be accomplished by either the oven or boiler method. When using the oven method, preheat to 220° - 245° F (104° - 118° C), and bake finely ground up flower for about 30 - 40 minutes, depending on the medicinal compounds you are planing to maximize. The boiling points of the different medicinal compounds, cannabinoids, terpenoids, and flavonoids, are laid out in Chapter 4 : Trichomes, Terps, & Temps. Another method used by Canna Chefs is the boiler method. In this method, again finely ground up your cannabis flower and place in a vacuum-sealed bag. Submerge the finely ground bagged cannabis into boiling water between 60 - 90 minutes. After allowed time, remove bag from water and allow to cool before opening.

• Rather using the oven method or the water bath method, be sure to moderate the temperature throughout the process.

With this simple breakdown you should be able accomplish the decarboxylation process, activating desired medicinal compounds, as well as having the ability to dose yourselves around your desired level with Deliciously Dee's delicious cannabis-infused recipes. Use your best judgement to how much cannabis-infused edibles you consume.

Also note that these doses are the Deliciously Dee™ recommended doses for different tolerance levels.

1 - 10 milligrams (mg) LOW mg tolerance
for low-mid pain, non-users or occasional users

10 - 30 milligrams (mg) MEDIUM mg tolerance
for the mid pain level tolerances

30 - + milligrams (mg) HIGH mg tolerance
for high pain levels, experienced users

As a patient it is important for you to figure out on your own by carefully measuring your dose and determine the best dose for your body. I strongly recommend all consumers to educate themselves on what is the active ingredient(s) in the medicine before consuming. Cannabinoids activate specific receptors found throughout the body to produce a pharmacologic effect. Mainly in the central and immune system.

I urge all patients to consult their physicians regarding the benefits of eating verse inhaling cannabis.

Even for experienced smokers, digesting edibles is an entirely different experience. When smoking cannabis, not all of the active medicine will get into the bloodstream because it gets lost as smoke/vapor/residue etc that does not get inhaled. When inhaling cannabis smoke, the effects happen practically instant. This makes it easier for the consumer to judge if they need more to get to their desired level of medication. With cooking and medicating with edibles, everything in what you eat gets digested into the body. Most edibles, after consuming, are digested and then processed through the liver before entering the blood stream. This turns delta-9- tetrahydrocannabinol into 11-hydroxy-tetrahydrocannabinol.

THC

11-Hydroxy-THC

11- Hydroxy - Tetrahydrocannabinol molecule

It is what happens to delta-9-tetrahydrocannabinol (THC) after it's processed through the liver which is the magic behind why edibles effect you the way they do and the longer lasting, medicinal effects. You are also not smoking, so there is no subsequent health risks to your respiratory system.

- After eating edibles, most will get impatient and will eat more. I strongly advise those to wait. While it is not yet documented as being physically possible for oneself to overdose on cannabis. The effects from eating to much cannabis, or over intoxication, can be most unpleasant.

<u>Possible Effects of Over Consumption</u>
Passing out/Sleepy
Feeling sick/Nauseated - vomiting
Disoriented
Unable to talk
Unable to move - "couch lock"
Coordination is highly affected so do NOT operate ANY heavy machinery or drive. *Remember - Drive When You Drive.*

<u>A Deliciously Dee Tip</u> : If you are feeling any of these symptoms. Drink lots of fluid. Plenty of water and orange juice. High volume vitamin C is known to help aid in these occurrences. Also keep non-medicated food around for consuming - we have to satisfy those munchies.

<u>Another Tip</u> : When practicing each recipe to your desired dose. Make notes of exactly how much cannabis you are using to better help you master your recipe.

THE CHOICE IS YOURS

As always fresh is best and clean is FRESH! Be sure to purchase your medical cannabis at a dispensary or grow your own. There has been cases where patients with compromised immune systems consumed cannabis that had fungi or microbial contamination on the flower got dangerously ill - and can also be fatal. There has also been cases of patients inhaling pesticide covered cannabis. Please purchase your medicine and look for a certified lab test.

If you grow your own, you know what you are putting in your body. There are great resources on the web. If you research the name of the strain of cannabis you are cooking with you can easily find the compounds in and potency range for the medicine you grew.

In Deliciously Dee's professional opinion, the best forms of edibles for patients desiring a quicker effect, is to purchase at a dispensary or to make at home, hard candies, or lozenges - look for my Relax With Happy™ Ambers . Ambers, or lozenges, dissolve in your mouth first, entering the bloodstream sublingually, allowing for the medicinal effects to happen quicker.

Those of us at Deliciously Dee™ - The Happy Confections ™ are NOT responsible for any mis-educating. The following cannabis cooking methods and recipes are for educational purposes only. I strongly urge no one to do anything illegal. Also we do not know the quality of medicine you are using or your tolerance level. Please dose yourself the best to your knowledge

(Photo by Kayley Garrett)

V

Trichomes, Terps, & Temps

Trying to find the healthiest cooking oil matched with the boiling point of the medicinal compounds desired, is important. You want to cook with an oil that has a high flash (smoke) point while activating the medicinal properties of the cannabinoids, terpenoids and flavonoids found predominantly in the trichomes of the plant.

As we learned earlier there is more to cannabis medicine than delta-9-THC. So, in saying that, choosing your medical marijuana based solely on THC potency is like choosing a fine wine by its alcohol content. Make sure when choosing your medicine to look at all the medicinal components. In this chapter I educate on how to maximize the benefits of those compounds.

The definition of trichome is "a small hair or other outgrowth from the epidermis of a plant, algae, lichens, and certain protists, typically unicellular and glandular." Trichomes are the very factories that produce the known cannabinoids, terpenoids, and flavonoids that make different cannabis strains unique, potent, and effective!

These "hairs" exist in many shapes and sizes. The three that appear most often on cannabis plants are bulbous trichomes, capitate-sessile trichomes, and capitate-stalked trichomes.

The gland heads of the capitate-stalked trichomes serves as the epicenter for terpenoid and cannabinoid synthesis. These glands may be seen by the naked eye while the bulbous and capitate-sessile trichomes can be as small as 10-15 micrometers and therefore only can be seen under a microscope. The Greek word"Trichoma," meaning "cover with hair," is where the Trichomes name originated.

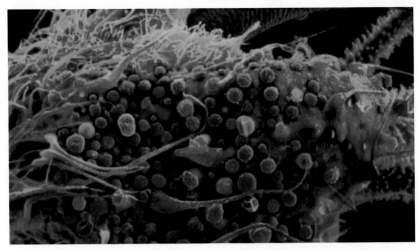

(Photo : Cannabis under a microscope taken at DigiPath Labs Las Vegas, NV)

However, it is now used amongst my work associates and myself as the term - what some of y'all call "couch lock"- we call a "Tri-COMA"!

**There you go, if I was getting too science for you guys …I threw in a joke. (:

To extract is to remove a substance or activate with desirable properties that are from the tissue of the plant and then discarding the unwanted, inactive plant matter. It is usually, especially in a lab-production setting, treated with a solvent (CO_2, Butane, Ethanol - Alcohol). However, this chapter is to educate you on infusion, an extract prepared by soaking the leaves of a plant or herb in liquid (oils, butters, etc) properly to maximize the most medicinal properties this plant has to offer. A safer method for "the happy chefs" at home.

**WARNING : When cooking with canna at home you should have separate cookware as your "infusion-ware" from your normal every day cooking set. Cannabis Oil - ESPECIALLY ones extracted with a solvent (CO_2, Butane, Ethanol) - sticks to stainless steel and majority of pots and pans surfaces.

Meaning, unless you soak and clean removing the extracted decarboxylated oil from surfaces with high proof ethanol, that oil remains on the surface of the cookware. In knowing that, with the reheating of the pot in a later use you will be slightly infusing your next dish - possibly many dishes - with marijuana.

Most of you are thinking, "So what!! That's awesome!" --- NO - if you have guests, which a majority of you do, or you have kids, it is NEVER OKAY to dose someone without their prior knowledge. People have jobs that require them to be unable to enjoy our favorite plant and their circumstances are to be respected. Safer to have a separate set when making your own medicine at home. Be A Good Patient.

The method to any plant extract is heat and time. So let's start by getting you familiar with temperatures and the boiling points of cannabinoids, terpenoids, and flavonoids.

(Photo by Kayley Garrett)

BOILING POINTS OF KNOWN CANNABINOID COMPOUNDS

Compound Name	Compound Type	Medical Properties	Concentration % Dry Weight	Boiling Point (C)	Bolling Point (F)
Tetrahydrocannabiarian (THCV)	cannabinoid	Analgesic Euphoriant	0.0-1.36%	220	428
delta-8-tetrahydrocannabinol (THC)	cannabinoid	Resembles delta-9-thc less psychoactive more stable Antiemetic	0.0-0.%	175-178	347-352.4
delta-9-tetrahydrocannabinol (THC)	cannabinoid	Euphoriant, analgesic, anti-inflammatory, antioxidant, antiemetic	0.1-25%	200	392
Cannabidiol (CBD)	cannabinoid	Anxiolytic, analgesic, antipsychotic, anti-inflammatory, antioxidant, antispasmodic	0.1-2.89%	160-180	320-356
Cannabigerols (CBG)	cannabinoid	Anti-inflammatory, antibiotic, anti fungal	0.3-1.15%	52	125.6
Cannabinol (CBN)	cannabinoid	Oxidation breakdown, product, sedatice, antibiotic	0.0-1.6%	185	365
Cannabichromenes (CBC)	cannabinoid	Anti-inflammatory, antibiotic, anti fungal	0.0-0.65%	220	428
Cannabindiol (CBDL)	cannabinoid	Antipsychotic, analgesic, anti-inflammatory, anti-neoplastic, chem-preventive	-		

BOILING POINTS OF KNOWN TERPENOID COMPOUNDS

Compound Name	Compound Type	Medical Properties	Concentratio n % Dry Weight	Boiling Point (C)	Bolling Point (F)
Pulegone	Terpenoid	Memory booster? AChE Inhibitor Sedative Antipyretic	0.001%	224	435.2

62

Compound Name	Compound Type	Medical Properties	Concentration % Dry Weight	Boiling Point (C)	Boiling Point (F)
Alfa-terpineol	Terpenoid	Sedative, Antibiotic, AChE inhibitor, Antioxidant, Antimalarial	0.02%	217-218	422.6-424.4
borneol	Terpenoid	Antibiotic	0.008%	200	410
Terpineol-4-ol	Terpenoid	AChE inhibitor, antibiotic	0.0004%	160-180	408.2
Linalool	Terpenoid	Sedative, Antidepressant, Anxiolytic, Immune potentiator	0.002%	52	388.4
D- limonene	Terpenoid	Cannabinoid agonist? Immune potenziato Antidepressant Antimutagenic	0.14%	185	350.6
1.8-cineole (eucalyptol)	Terpenoid	AChE inhibitor, Antibiotic, Increase cerebral blood flow, stimulant, antiviral, anti-inflamitory, antinociceptive	>0.001%	220	348.8
Delta-3-carene	Terpenoid	Anti-inflamitory	0.0004%	168	334.4
Beta-myrcene	Terpenoid	Anti-inflamitory, Antibiotic, Analgesic, antimtagenic	0.47%	166-168	330.8-334.4

A description of some of the common terpenes molecules in cannabis
(vary by strain)

alfa-pinene (pinene): pine odor, bronchodilators that opens the lungs to possibly improve THC absorption. Responsible for increasing focus, energy, and self-satisfaction.

beta-caryophyllene (caryophyllene): woody, sweet, clove taste responsible for anti-inflammatory and neuro-protective effects through CB2 receptor activation.

d-limonene (limonene): citrus scent and may possess anti-bacterial, anti-fungal, anti-depression, and anti-cancer abilities

63

beta-myrcene (myrcene): likely effects, intake of THC by brain cells to increase the overall effects of THC when ingested together.

linalool: floral smell that is believed to provide some anti-cancer effects as well as being known to cause intense sedation.

BOILING POINTS OF KNOWN FLAVONOID COMPOUNDS

Compound Name	Compound Type	Medical Properties	Concentration % Dry Weight	Boiling Point (C)	Bolling Point (F)
Quercetin	Flavonoid	Antioxidant, Antimutagenic, Antiviral, Antineoplastic	>0.1%	250	482
Cannaflavin A	Flavonoid	COX inhibitor, LO inhibitor	0.02%	182	359.6
Apienin	Flavonoid	Anxiolytic, Anti-inflammatory Estrogenic	.0.1%	178	352.4
Beta-sitosterol	Flavonoid	Anti-inflammatory 5-Alfa-reductase Inhibitor	?	119	246.2

BOILING POINTS OF KNOWN TOXINS

Compound Name	Compound Type	Medical Properties	Concentration % Dry Weight	Boiling Point (C)	Bolling Point (F)
Benzene	Toxin	Carcinogen	?	80.1	392
Carbon monoxide & smoke tars (At point of combustion)	Toxin	Carcinogen	?	230	482

With the known information of the boiling temperatures of the different types of cannabis compounds it would be safe to stay within the temperatures of 240° F - 320° F (115.5° C - 160° C). Staying within these ranges guarantees maximizing the medical properties of the plant during the decarboxylation process with the exception of cannabigerols CBG. CBG boiling point is 125.5° F (52° C) so if you are needing cannabigerols medicinal properties, you would to take down the temperature and cook for a longer period of time.

Cannabis begins to decarboxylate at around 220° Fahrenheit. For the optimal oven method, you should preheat to 220°-245°, and bake the ground-up flower for about 30-45 minutes, depending on your preferences and the cannabis being utilized.

I know some of y'all read that and may be thinking, "wait i thought THC boiling point is 314° F, that's what Wikipedia and other sources say..." and you would be correct. Many sources site Wikipedia as their go to for the "facts" and yes they can be a great source. However, it was recorded on PubChem.com the boiling point of delta-9-tetrahydrocannabinol as 392° F (200° C). What I have seen in my professional experience at the lab, is that the boiling point is noticeably higher than 315° F; I've observed it to be upwards of closer to 400° F.

Which makes since due to the vaporization temperatures to be believed ranging from 250° - 400° F. But also, staying in the 240° F - 320° F range allows maximum potency of the other compounds other than delta 9.

With this knowledge let's now choose the proper cooking oil for ourselves catered to our cooking habits and diets.

FLASH (SMOKE) POINTS OF COMMON COOKING OILS

Cooking Oils/Fats	Smoking Point (C)	Smoking Point (F)	Omega-6-Omega-3 Ratio (relevant fat information)
Unrefined Flax Seed Oil	107°	225°	1:4
Unrefined Safflower Oil	107°	225°	133:1
Unrefined Sunflower Oil	107°	225°	40:1
Unrefined Corn Oil	160°	320°	83:1
Unrefined High-oleic Sunflower Oil	160°	320°	40:1 (84% mono saturated)
Extra Virgin Olive Oil	160°	320°	73% (monounsaturated, high in Omega 9)
Unrefined Peanut Oil	160°	320°	32:1
Semi Refined Safflower Oil	160°	320°	133:1 (75% Omega 9)
Unrefined Soy Oil	160°	320°	8:1 (most are GMO)
Hemp Seed Oil	165°	330°	3:1
Unrefined Walnut Oil	160°	320°	5:1
Butter	177°	350°	9:1 (mostly saturated & mono saturated)
Semi Refined Canola Oil	177°	350°	2:1 (56% Omega 9, 80% Canola is GMO)
Coconut Oil	177°	350°	86% healthy saturated, lurid acid (has antibac antioxidant, and antiviral properties)
Unrefined sesame Oil	177°	350°	138:1
Semi Refined Soy Oil	177°	350°	8:1

Cooking Oils/Fats	Smoking Point (C)	Smoking Point (F)	Omega-6-Omega-3 Ratio (relevant fat information)
Vegetable Shortening	182°	360°	Most unhealthy saturated, Trans Fat
Lard	182°	360°	Most unhealthy saturated, Trans Fat
Refined Canola Oil	204°	400°	3:1 (80% of canola in US is GMO)
High Quality (low acidity) Extra Virgin Olive Oil	207°	405°	13:1 (74% mono saturated, 71.3% Omega 9)
Sesame oil	210°	410°	42:1
Cottonseed Oil	216°	420°	54:1
Grapeseed Oil	216°	420°	676:1 (12% saturated, 17% mono saturated)
Virgin Olive Oil	216°	420°	13:1 (74% mono saturated, 71.3% Omega 9)
Almond Oil	216°	420°	Omegas-6
Hazelnut Oil	221°	430°	75% mono saturated (no Omega 3, 78% Omega
Peanut Oil	227°	440°	32:1
Sunflower Oil	227°	440°	40:1
Refined Corn Oil	232°	450°	83:1
Palm Oil	232°	450°	46:1 (mostly saturated & mono saturated)
Palm Kernel Oil	232°	450°	83:1
Refined High-oleic Sunflower Oil	232°	450°	39:1 (84% mono saturated)
Refined Peanut Oil	232°	450°	32:1
Semi Refined Sesame Oil	232°	450°	138:1
Refined Soy Oil	232°	450°	8:1 (most GMO)
Semi Refined Sunflower Oil	232°	450°	40:1
Olive Pomace Oil	238°	460°	(74% mono saturated, high in Omega 9)
Extra Light Olive Oil	242°	468°	(74% mono saturated, high in Omega 9)
Rice Bran Oil	254°	490°	21:1 (good source of vitamin E & antioxidants)
Refined Safflower Oil	266°	510°	133:1 (74% Omega 9)
Avocado Oil	271°	520°	12:1 (mono saturated, 68% Omega 9 fatty acids, High vitamin E)

**It is important to know the smoke point of oils because heating oil to the point where oil begins to smoke produces harmful free radicals and toxic fumes.

It is better to use a cooking oil that has a healthy balance of antioxidants, vitamins, and Omega-3 to Omega-6 fatty acids. Bottom line is that when possible, buy and use organic, unrefined, cold-processed vegetable oils. DO NOT use extra virgin olive oil for high temperature cooking, but rather in salads or to add to cooked foods.

<u>Deliciously Dee Oil Preferences</u>
extra virgin olive oil (low temp cooking)
coconut oil (mid temp cooking)
extra light olive oil (mid - high temp cooking)
avocado oil (high temp cooking)

For low temperature cooking I use extra virgin olive oil. It's best to choose oils with a higher Omega-3 fatty acids, they promote healthy cellular function and decrease stroke and heart attack risk. They are also known for their anti-inflammatory properties - which match and combine nicely with the medicinal benefits of the cannabis compounds.

Your body also needs Omega-6 fatty acids to maintain cell wall integrity and to provide energy to the heart. Although your body needs Omega-6 acids, too much of these can increase inflammation in the body. As see in the earlier charts; cannabinoids, terpenoids, flavonoids, and many vegetable oils have anti-inflammatory properties to possibly counteract ingesting too much Omega-6 in the body - it is still best to keep an eye on your intake.

For high-temperature cooking I use avocado oil. Avocado oil is high in Omega-9. Omega-9 fatty acids are considered to be "conditionally essential," which means that although your body produces them, they aren't produced in meaningful quantities. Consuming Omega-9 fatty acids, such as oleic acid lowers the risk of heart disease, athero-sclerosis, and aids in cancer prevention. It is always best to look for organic, cold-processed oil. *Extra virgin olive oil and Extra light olive oil are also high in Omega-9.

You can use coconut oil for most mid-temperature cook-ing, which is high in beneficial saturated fats and medium chain triglycerides. Also containing anti-viral, antibacterial, anti-fungal and antioxidant properties - which again pairs nicely with the benefits of our cannabis compounds. To add another Fun Fact...! Coconut oil is just simply amaz-ing! It is probably my absolute favorite as it sustains many uses. Coconut oil is very beneficial for your body: teeth, hair, nails, skin... It is an essential and required ingredient in my kitchen for making THC, CBD infused topicals: lo-tions, salves, massage oils, and lubricants. I urge you all to do some research on the benefits of coconut oil and add it your daily routine and diet.

(Photo by Kayley Garrett)

Canna Cooking Oils

(COCONUT OIL, OLIVE OIL, VEGETABLE OIL, ETC)

INGREDIENTS

4 cups oil

AND <u>ONE</u> OF THE NEXT THREE*

1/2 oz of flower cannabis   (low mg tolerance)
3/4 oz pf flower cannabis   (medium mg tolerance)
1 oz of cannabis   (high mg tolerance)

*high tolerance is best for high tolerance pain levels. Consult your physician about dosing.

First, pour whatever oil you decide to use into a large skillet. (you may also use the double boiler method or slow cooker) Put your stove top on a medium-low heat setting. Let it warm up... do not let it boil... this is very important for quality cannabis oil. Now, once your oil is hot, you may add your finely ground raw cannabis into the skillet.

Turn down the heat so that it is just below simmering. Make sure you stir frequently and watch out for boiling... do not let it come to a boil (bubbles are bad - if you start to see any bubbling remove from heat) and let it cool down.

You are going to continue this for the next 60 - 90 minutes, stirring frequently. Every few minutes take the wooden spoon and dip it in oil and make a dot on a white plate (or napkin). You will see the oil go from a clear to dark green. You want it at a good shade of green. Do not cook for more than 2 hours - as you risk over decarboxylation and scorching.

Now, after around 60 - 90 minutes. Turn off heat and the let oil cool down... let it cool enough so that you do not burn yourself. Then, grab a cheesecloth or a metal strainer and strain to remove infused oil from plant matter. Pour into an airtight container of your choice - I use mason jars! You may also put in the freezer for a longer shelf life.

- When cooking with cannabis, the oil is very sticky and will stick to your cookware. Using specified cookware just for preparing your medicine, using silicon and pyrex dishes are also preferred as oil doesn't stick. Remember, too, when infusing your canna oil, budder, and milk in the following chapters - you can always dilute the potency by adding un-medicated or un-infused oil, butter, or milk to your recipe. Get to YOUR comfortable level of happiness!

VII

Canna Budder

INGREDIENTS:

4 sticks (1 lb) unsalted butter

AND <u>ONE</u> OF THE NEXT THREE

1/2 oz of cannabis   (low mg tolerance)
3/4 oz of cannabis (medium mg tolerance)
1 oz of cannabis   (high mg tolerance)

high tolerance is best for high tolerance pain levels. Consult your physician about dosing.

(use a coffee grinder to finely ground your dried cannabis)

METHOD :

First, melt the butter in double boiler or slow cooker until it is melted or at a low simmer. Then, after grounding up cannabis, add to pan slowly while stirring, for about 45 minutes to an hour. Make sure you stir frequently. Let simmer , the butter will begin to bubble at surface and you will notice it turning a green hue - therefore turning into BUDDER.

Next pour the budder through your metal strainer or cheese cloth to remove excess plant matter . Make sure to put pressure or squeeze the remaining budder out of cooked w cannabis as much as possible. Lastly, place in fridge and let chill until it becomes solid. You may also keep in freezer until use for longer shelf life.

- When cooking with cannabis, the oil is very sticky and will stick to your cookware. Using specified cookware just for cooking your medicine, using silicon and pirex dishes are also preferred as oil doesn't stick. Remember, also, when infusing your canna oil, budder, and milk in the following chapters - you can always dilute the potency by adding unmedicated or un-infused oil, butter, or milk to your recipe. Get to YOUR comfortable level of happiness!

VIII

Mary's Milk

Prep: 15min   Cook: 45min   Happy: 60min

INGREDIENTS:

1 cup of milk or cream
1/8 (3.5g) ground cannabis

for each cup of milk use 1/8 cup ground cannabis

First, take the 1/8 of chopped cannabis and place it in your handy dandy coffee grinder because you must get the cannabis ground as fine as possible. Next pour your milk into a saucepan and heat until it comes to a simmer. When it begins to slightly bubble, begin to stir the cannabis in slowly and lower the heat. Allow this to simmer for about an hour.

*Keep watch on it as milk can easily over flow if there is too much heat. Make sure to stir frequently and stay close by. When the hour passes, let the milk cool down. Then , grab your cheese cloth and strain milk into air tight container of your choice. (I prefer mason jars)

Make sure you strain it well so there are no cannabis plant matter remains left in liquid. Date your Mary Milk and keep refrigerated! Get Happy!

- *When cooking with cannabis, the oil is very sticky and will stick to your cookware. Using specified cookware just for cooking your medicine, using silicon and pirex dishes are also preferred as oil doesn't stick. Remember, also, when infusing your canna oil, budder, and milk in the following chapters - you can always dilute the potency by adding unmedicated or un-infused oil, butter, or milk to your recipe. Get to YOUR comfortable level of happiness!*

Deliciously Happy

A collection of infused dishes,
for those who enjoy a happier taste pallet.

Happy Gummies

Makes 350 chews depending on molds.

YOU WILL NEED:

2 small pots/saucepans
2 candy thermometers
spoons
baster
gummy molds (your preference)
* corn starch as needed over molds.

INGREDIENTS:

1/2 cup gelatin powder
1 cup water
1 1/4 cups sugar
2 tbsp sorbitol (powder form)
3/4 cup corn syrup
1 tbsp citric acid
1 dram of flavor
6-10 drops of food color

1/4 cup cannabis infused coconut oil
OR sub un-infused coconut oil and add
- 1 gram of decarboxylated cannabis oil
corn starch as needed

PART ONE - GELATIN SOLVENT:
* In separate pot, make a water bath with a candy thermometer keeping temperature around 150° F.
- 1/2 cup gelatin
- 1 cup water

Both ingredients in a zip lock bag. Mix thoroughly, removing clumps and streaks. Cook in water bath for 20 - 30 minutes until clear.

PART TWO - SUGAR SOLVENT:
- 1 1/4 cup sugar
- 2 tbsp sorbitol (powder form)
3/4 cup corn syrup
1/4 cup infused coconut oil

OR sub un-infused coconut oil and add

- 1 gram of decarbed CANNA OIL
Mix ingredients well, when sugar and sorbitol have dissolved (around 10 minutes) add your decarbed

CANNA OIL to the pot. Mix well! Continue cooking for 20 minutes.

PART THREE - COMBINE:

Coat your molds thoroughly with corn starch.

Combine PART ONE to PART TWO.

Add your food color, citric acid, and flavor of choice.

*Add 6-10 drops for a good hue.

Mix well! Collect with baster and (this will take a "flick of the wrist" so to speak) put in desired mold quickly. Let stand in molds for 6+ hours. (preferably over night)

Then....HAPPY time!

Happy Candied Rope

YOU WILL NEED:

2 small pots/saucepans
2 candy thermometers
spoons
2 7" x 11" baking tray
parchment paper
knife
corn starch as needed over molds.

INGREDIENTS:

1/2 cup gelatin powder
1 cup water
1 1/4 cups sugar
2 tbsp sorbitol (powder form)
3/4 cup corn syrup
1 tbsp citric acid
1 dram of flavor
6-10 drops of food color

3 6oz. boxes of nerd candy
1/4 cup cannabis infused coconut oil

OR sub un-infused coconut oil and add
- 1 gram of decarboxylated cannabis oil
corn starch as needed

PART ONE - GELATIN SOLVENT:

* In separate pot, make a water bath with a candy thermometer keeping temperature around 150° F.

- 1/2 cup gelatin
- 1 cup water

Both ingredients in a zip lock bag. Mix thoroughly, removing clumps and streaks. Cook in water bath for 20 - 30 minutes until clear.

PART TWO - SUGAR SOLVENT:

- 1/4 cup sugar
3/4 cup corn syrup
1/4 cup infused coconut oil

OR sub un-infused coconut oil and add - 1 gram of

decarbed CANNA OIL.

Mix ingredients well, when sugar has dissolved (around 10 minutes) add CANNA OIL to the pot. Mix well! Continue cooking for 20 minutes.

PART THREE - COMBINE:

Combine PART ONE to PART TWO. Add your food color, citric acid, and flavor of choice.

*Add 6-10 drops for a good hue. Mix well! Let the mixture set awhile 25 - 30 minutes, until it thickens, viscous. (pourable, not watery)

Place parchment paper in baking tray, covering all sides. Coat the parchment lightly with corn starch. Pour the mixture into tray or if you are comfortable with the viscous consistency of your mixture you may pour the mixture right on to the parchment allowing it to pool, but not be too much of a liquid consistency to not stay on sheet.

Let mixture set 5 - 10 minutes on parchment.

Grab the other baking tray. Place the parchment paper covering the bottom of the baking tray. Fill tray with nerds.

Take your "slab" of gummy mixture and slice into desired sized ropes.

Roll the ropes in your pool of nerds. - HAPPY time!

(Photo by Kayley Garrett)

Ambers

Makes 150-200 hard candies. (depending on molds you are using)

HAPPY NOTE: Hard candy is hard to make, you have to move quickly. It is strongly recommended to do multiple test batches.

YOU WILL NEED:

1 medium pot/saucepan
1 candy thermometers
1 silicone spatula
*desired silicone candy molds

INGREDIENTS:

1 cup water
3/4 cups corn syrup
2 cups granulated sugar
4 ml decarboxylated cannabis oil
4-10 drops of desired food coloring
1 dram of desired flavor

DIRECTIONS:

Make sure your silicone candy molds are close by, cleaned and ready.

Pour corn syrup, sugar and water into a medium size pot on the stove at high heat. Mix ingredients well and place a candy thermometer attaching to side of the pan. Let temperature rise. *It is important to watch temperature closely as the hardening effect depends solely on reaching correct temperature.

Once thermometer reaches 250° Farenhiet, pour 4 grams of cannabis oil in pot. Let the boiling mix the oil in batch without stirring.

As the thermometer rises to 300° F, watch thermometer closely. Remove pot from heat once temperature reaches 315° F. Pour in food coloring and desired flavor. Stir mixture with a silicone spatula until color is even.

Pour mixture while it's still a hot liquid into molds evenly. Be careful, but also move quickly as mixture is hot and will harden fast.
Let set for 15 minutes. Place mold in freezer to harden for one hour.
Crack candies out of molds and get Happy! (:

Happy Butter Cups

makes around 25 - 50 units (depends on cups size)

YOU WILL NEED:

double boiler
piping bags
rolling pin
hand mixer
molds/paper cup liners

INGREDIENTS:

2 cups of chocolate chips (your preference)
1 cup peanut butter (or almond butter)
1/2 cup graham crackers
1.2 grams decarboxylated cannabis oil

DIRECTIONS:

In a double boiler, throw your chocolate chips in on medium low heat (110° - 130° F).

Now while the chocolate is melting, grab the graham crackers and your rolling pin and crush until the grahams are now crumbs.

In a separate bowl, spoon out the peanut butter and blend in the graham crumbs. Put mixture into a piping bag and set aside.

Once the chocolate has melted, throw in your CANNA OIL and mix with your hand mixer thoroughly for around 8 - 10 minutes.

Take your molds and with the infuse chocolate at a layer to the bottom of the mold or cup, tilt the mold so that the chocolate drips and evenly coats all sides. You may want to tap the mold lightly on the counter to evenly flatten the layer of chocolate. Let set (harden) for about 30 minutes. * You may pop the into freezer for a quicker set time.

Now that the bottom and sides are done. Grab your piping bag, cut the tip off of the end and begin dispensing the peanut butter graham mixture into the hollow, filling almost to the top. (make sure to leave room for the top layer of chocolate.

Lastly, top each unit with a layer of chocolate. Tap the mold lightly to get the layer to flatten nicely and then your peanut butter cups are capped.

Happy Covered Oreos

Makes 40 units

YOU WILL NEED:

double boiler
hand mixer
molds

INGREDIENTS:

2 1/2 cups of chocolate chips (your preferenc
1 package of Oreo Cookies
3 grams decarboxylated cannabis oil

DIRECTIONS:

In a double boiler, throw your chocolate chips in on medium low heat (110° - 130° F).

Once the chocolate has melted, throw in your CANNA OIL and mix with your hand mixer thoroughly for around 8-10 minutes. Take your molds and with the infuse chocolate at a layer to the bottom of the mold, tilt the mold so that the chocolate drips and evenly coats the bottom and all sides.

You may want to tap the mold lightly on the counter to evenly flatten the layer of chocolate. Let set (harden) for about 20 minutes.

Now that the bottom and sides are done. Grab your Oreo cookies and add a cookie   covering each bottom layer of the chocolate.

Lastly, top each cookie filled unit with a layer of chocolate. Fill around the perimeter of cookie well, making sure there are no air bubbles. Tap the mold lightly to get the layer to flatten nicely and then let set for 25-30 minutes. (pop in freezer for faster set time)

(:

Devil's Harvest Bars

INGREDIENTS:

1 1/2 cup flour
1 1/3 cup rolled oats
1 cup brown sugar
3/4 tsp baking soda
1/2 tsp salt
12 tbsp , melted and cooled butter
12 oz dark chocolate chips
40 soft easy melt caramel candies
6 tbsp cannabis infused heavy cream
almonds - shaved (desired amount)

DIRECTIONS :

Preheat the oven to 350° Fahrenheit . Combine the flour, oats, sugar, baking soda, and salt in a large bowl. Melt the butter, let it cool, and pour into the mixing bowl with the dry ingredients. Stir (i use a wooden spoon) until a soft dough forms. It should be just slightly crumbly. If the dough feels wet and heavy, add a little more flour.

Press 3/4 of the dough into a 9x13 baking dish. Reserve the remaining 1/4 for topping. Bake for 13 minutes or until the top is barely golden brown.

While crust is baking. Unwrap caramels and melt in microwave with the infused heavy cream. Stir until the mixture is smooth and pourable.

Sprinkle chocolate chips over the baked crust. Pour melted caramel over the chocolate chips. Crumble the remaining dough with your fingers (add a little more flour if it's not crumbly enough) and sprinkle over the top of the bars. Bake for another 15 - 20 minutes, until the top layer is golden brown. Let stand for several hours or until the caramel us cooled. Get Happy!

Almond Budder Cookies

Ingredients:

1/2 Cup of Budder
1 1/2 Cups Granulated Sugar
1 1/2 Cups Brown Sugar
4 Eggs
1 Tsp Vanilla
2 Cups Chunky Almond Butter (or peanut butter)
6 Cups Quick and old fashion Oats
2 1/2 Tsp Baking Soda
Cranberries

DIRECTIONS :

First, Beat together budder and sugars. Blend in eggs and vanilla. Add almond butter (peanut butter). Mix well. Stir in oats and baking soda. Put rounded table- spoonfuls on baking sheet. Arrange cranberries on top of cookies. Bake 375 F for 10 min.

(You can add cranberries in dough instead of adding to cookies on top later.)

Canna Crispy Treats

Preheat Oven to: 375 F

Ingredients:

1lb Budder
10 Cups Rice Crispy Cereal
20 oz Mini Marshmallows
1 Tbsp Corn Starch

DIRECTIONS :

First, take your budder in your double boiler and melt it down at about 170 F. Stay at this temperature and begin to melt and mix all of your marshmallows. It will look runny because of the budder, this is where you throw in the cornstarch. Mix in your cornstarch. Then, as to your liking add more marshmallows.

Lastly, add your cereal to a large mixing bowl, Pour the marshmallow weed mixture over, and mix well. Let your treats cool down. Then, Spread out evenly over a wax paper. Then, cut into shapes and squares of your taste. Serve. Yummy!

Happy Zucchini Bread

Prep: 20min

Cook: 60min

Happy: 1hr 40min

INGREDIENTS :

3 cups all-purpose flour
1 cup CANNABIS INFUSED vegetable oil
2 1/4 cups white sugar
2 cups grated zucchini
1 cup chopped walnuts
3 eggs
1 tablespoon ground cinnamon *See benefits below.
3 teaspoons vanilla extract
1 teaspoon salt
1 teaspoon baking soda

DIRECTIONS :

Grease and flour two 8 x 4 inch pans. reheat oven to 325 degrees F (165 degrees C)

Sift flour, salt, baking soda, and cinnamon together in a bowl.

Beat eggs, oil, vanilla, and sugar together in a large bowl. Add sifted ingredients to the creamed mixture, and beat well. Stir in zucchini and nuts until well combined. Pour batter into prepared pans.

Bake for 40 to 60 minutes, or until tester inserted in the center comes out clean. Cool in pan on rack for 20 minutes. Remove bread from pan, and completely cool.

B-Real's Banana Bud Bread

INGREDIENTS :

1/2 cup budder
2 cups flour (for higher tolerances sub w cannaflour)
3 Bananas (ripe)
1/2 cup milk
1 cup sugar
2 Eggs
1 Tsp Baking Soda
1/2 Tsp Vanilla Extract

DIRECTIONS

First, preheat oven to 350 F degrees. Beat the budder, eggs, milk, and sugar in a large bowl. Next, add baking soda and vanilla. Add flour slowly while beating. After all is mixed, add the bananas and beat until mostly smashed. Place in a greased glass baking dish and bake for one hour.

Deliciously Dee's Pot Brownies

(Vegan/ Vegetarian Friendly)

INGREDIENTS :

1/8 Finely Ground Cannabis (use coffee grinder)
1 Cup Cannabis Oil
2 Cups Flour
2 Cups Brown Sugar
1 1/2 Cups Water
1 Tsp Baking Powder
1 Tsp Vanilla
1/2 Cup Chocolate & White Chocolate Chips

DIRECTIONS

First, Grab a large skillet put your cannabis oil on low heat for a minute or so. Next, add the finely ground cannabis, stir for about 30 minutes on a low simmer. Next, mix all the dry ingredients in a large mixing bowl. Next, over mixing bowl with your dry ingredients...time to get them wet!

Place a strainer bowl over top and pour your cannabis oil with weed through strainer so all oil gets into bowl. Leaving all weed pieces in strainer. Next you add the rest of the ingredients and mix. Bake in a greased 7x11 baking dish for 20-28 minutes. Let cool. Enjoy!

Proper dose is about a 2x2 square.

Lazy Man's Pot Brownies

(Not Vegan/ Vegetarian Friendly)

DIRECTIONS :

First, go to any grocery store... one closest to your house preferably. Pick out any box of your favorite brownies. Make sure recipe calls for oil. Now follow the recipe exactly how it says on the box except where it says vegetable oil, substitute your cannabis oil.

Bake as directed and get happy!

OG Garlic Shrimp

Prep: 15min

Cook: 25min

Happy: 40min

INGREDIENTS:

2 dozen (large) fresh shrimp
1/4 cup infused olive oil
1/4 cup (chopped) fresh parsley
3 cloves (minced) garlic
1/2 teaspoon pepper
1/4 cup canna butter
1/2 cup (toast them ish) french breadcrumbs
3/4 cup freshly grated parmesan cheese

DIRECTIONS :

First, peel shrimp, arrange in 11 by 7 inch baking dish. Pour oil all over shrimp.

Combine parsley and next 3 ingredients. Sprinkle over shrimp.

Cover and bake at 300° F for 15 minutes.

Then, turn Shrimp over...drizzle w BUDDER and sprinkle w breadcrumbs and cheese. Bake uncovered 5 to 10 minutes. Serve!

P-Funk Wings

I dedicate this recipe to my friend Benzel Baltimore (The Funky Drummer) and George Clinton and the Parliament Funkadelic!

Servings: 8
1 serving = 4 wings

INGREDIENTS :

5 lbs chicken wings (washed/cleaned)
1/2 cup butter

*preferably cut the wings separating the drumette from the wingette and cut and remove the tips.

DIRECTIONS :

Preheat oven to 420° F (210° C). Place 1/2 cup butter in large bowl and set out to soften. If so desired, cut the wings separating the wingette from the drumette and cut and remove the tips. Dip wings in softened butter. Arrange wings on a cooling sheet that can be set inside the baking sheet. Cook the wings in preheated oven for 45 minutes to 1 hour, or until crisp and cooked through. After cooked and crisped, toss in one of my infused Deliciously Dee's Bauce Sauces below!

Hot Bauce Sauce

INGREDIENTS :

1 clove garlic (mince)
kosher salt
1/4 canna budder
1/4 cup chipotle hot sauce
1 tbsp corn starch

DIRECTIONS :

First, in a skillet, melt down your budder. Then add your favorite HOT sauce, garlic, and kosher salt. Stir well. Add 1 tbsp of corn starch stir until sauce begins to thicken. Done!

With sauces takes no more than 3 - 4 tsp for a good dose as per my Canna Budder recipe. Use for dipping or basting-- All Sauces must be kept in fridge.

BBQ Bauce Sauce

INGREDIENTS :

1/3 cup canna oil (infused olive oil)
3 tbsp green onions (finely chopped)

1 lime juiced
1 tbsp water
2 tbsp apple cider vinegar
2 tbsp worcesterhire sauce
1 tbsp soy sauce
3/4 cup tomato paste
1 tbsp garlic (minced)
2 tbsp brown sugar
1/2 tbsp chili powder
1 1/2 tbsp honey
1/3 cup pineapple juice
1/4 cup water

DIRECTIONS :

Grab your crock pot and set to 200° F. Throw in canna oil, green onions, squeezed lime, and water - cook for about an 90 minutes. Then, add the Worcestershire sauce, soy sauce, apple cider vinegar, garlic, tomato paste, brown sugar, honey, pineapple juice, and water. Stir and mix all ingredients well. Set at a simmer or on medium for another 40 - 50 minutes. Stir occasionally.

8 Layer Taco Dip

Ingredients:

1lb Sausage
1 Can (16oz) Refried Beans
1 Package Taco Seasoning Mix
2 1/2 Cups Shredded Mexican Cheeses
1 Carton Sour Cream (16oz)
1 Can (4.5 oz) Chopped Chilies
1 Can Diced Tomatoes
1 Can (6oz) Sliced Black Olives
1 Bunch of Green Onions Chopped
1 Jar (10oz) Medium Salsa (or mild if you are a wuss)
1 1/2 Cups Dr Greenthumb's Guacamole
(see previous page for recipe.)
2 Bags of Tortilla Chips
(Because 1 isn't enough, we know dis)

DIRECTIONS :

First, Grab a large skillet, cut and cook sausage until it is browned then drain the sausage. Then, stir in the beans, chillies, and taco seasoning mix. Next, grab a 7 by 11 serving dish and spread sausage mix. Top sausage mix with sour cream, salsa, and Dr. Greenthumb's Guacamole spread evenly (gotta make it green). Then sprinkle olives, tomatoes and onions on top. Lastly, cover with cheese. Serve with a big bowl of chips, and refrigerate and leftovers.

Cannabis Clam Dip

Ingredients:

1/2 Cup of Budder
1 Med Onion (Finely Chopped)
1/2 Green Pepper (Chopped into Small Pieces)
1 Tsp Olive Oil
1 Tsp Chopped Parsley
1 Tsp Lemon Juice
1 Tsp Oregano
1/2 Cup Bread Crumbs
2 Cans Chopped Clams With Their Juice
Swiss Cheese (Grated)

DIRECTIONS :

Melt budder in pan and lightly saute' onion and green pepper. Mix together with remaining ingredients, except Swiss Cheese, and place in a oven- proof baking dish. Top with Swiss Cheese and cover. Bake for 20-25 minutes. Remove from oven and serve with crackers of your choice.

Art-I-Choke Toke Dip

Ingredients:

\1 Cup Mayo (8oz)
1 Cup Sour Cream
1 Tbsp Finely Ground Cannabis
1 Cup Grated Parmesan Cheese
Tabasco for Taste
2 Cans Finely Chopped Artichokes Heart
(Plain Not Marinated)

2 Bags of Chips (Your Choice)

DIRECTIONS :

Mix all together in an oven-safe baking dish. Bake for 20 minutes.

Remove from oven.

Place in serving bowl.

Served with chips, bread or whatever makes you happy!

Motherships Chicken Dip

Ingredients:

1 Large Can White Chix Meat
1 12oz Cream Cheese Softened
1 Can Cream of Chix Soup
1/4 Cup Finely Ground Cannabis
Jalapeños (Many as you like)

2 Bags of Chips (Your Choice)

DIRECTIONS :

First, drain chicken meat- Place in bowl with next 4 ingredients and place in small crock pot. Stir frequently. After an hour of cooking and stirring, it should be hot enough to serve!

(Told you that you may want different sizes)

Set on low and serve with a bowl of chips or breads cut for dipping.

Mary-juana Poppas

Ingredients:

12 Jalapeño Peppers
2 Tbsp Cannabis Oil
1/3 Cup Green Onions, White Parts Only (Chopped)
2 Cloves Garlic, Minced
1 Block Cream Cheese Softened

DIRECTIONS :

First, cut off tops of the jalapeños. Clean out as much of the inside as possible. You want the peppers to be hollow for stuffing. Rinse out the inside of the pepper with water. Next, warm a small saucepan over medium heat and add your cannabis oil. Let the oil warm for about 30 seconds, then add the green onions and cook for about 1 minute. Then, throw in the garlic and saute' for 1 to 2 minutes. next, remove and add the cream cheese and stir. The sauce should be kinda thick

Now to stuff da stuff: Use a spoon and fingers (get messy) and fill the peppers with your stoner stuffing. Lastly, placed stuff peppers on a foil-lined baking sheet and bake for 20 minutes. Serve warm.

It's Gravy Baby

(Sauces take no more than 3 to 4 tablespoons for a good dose to get high. Use for dipping or basting-- All sauces must be kept in fridge.)

Ingredients:

2 Cups of Turkey, Chicken, or Vegetable Stock
1/3 Cup of Cannaflour
2 White Onions (Sliced)
2 Tbsp of Sage
1/2 Cup Balsamic Vinegar
2 Tbsp Fresh Rosemary (Chopped)
6 Tbsp of Budder
Salt & Pepper to Taste

DIRECTIONS :

First, Grab a large skillet, set on medium, and throw in your budder. Cook at a simmer. Saute' onions for about 10 minutes. Throw in the fresh Sage and Rosemary, then cook another 10 minutes. Add Vinegar. While doing so, slowly add in your cannaflour and begin whisking. Add in whichever stock you decide to use. Keep whisking until the lumps are gone and the sauce begins to thicken. Add salt and pepper for tasting

WARNING: Please use your judgment in your tolerance as everyone is different. There is weed contained in this recipe. There are no standard strengths or doses so quantities might not be approximate.

German Ganja POTato Salad

Ingredients:

5 Med Potatoes
1/2 Cup Chopped Onions
1/2 Cup Vinegar
1/2 Cup Water
3 Tbsp Finely Ground Cannabis
1 1/2 Tsp Salt
1 Tsp Pepper

DIRECTIONS :

Boil Potatoes with skin on (I like red potatoes) Meanwhile in large saucepan put onions to fry and mix together vinegar, water, cannabis, sugar, salt and pepper. Cook till well blended...Mix well gently then crumble bacon on top.

Note: Love serving with Bratwursts!

Maryjane Meatballs

Ingredients:

3 Lbs Italian Meatballs
1 (16oz) Can Whole Berry Cranberry Sauce
1 (12oz) Bottle of Chili Sauce
1/4 Cup finely Ground Cannabis
1 Tbsp Lemon Juice
1/4 Cup Brown Sugar

DIRECTIONS :

Mix all ingredients together in crock pot. Add Meatballs and cook on high for 1 hour, then turn down and cook on low for 4 hours.

Note: You can use turkey meat balls

Chronic Veal Scallopini

Ingredients:

4 4oz Veal Cutlets
4 Slices Prosciutto (about 4oz)
3 oz Fontina Cheese, Cut into 4 Slices
Salt & Pepper to taste
1/2 Cup All Purpose Cannaflour
1 Tbsp Budder
1 Tbsp Cannabis Oil 1 Cup Dry rWhite Wine

(Mudder recipe & a Happy Chef fave)

**Extremely High Dose: If you want to make less potent use
either the budder "or" the oil.**

DIRECTIONS :

Between wax paper pound veal to 1/8" thickness. Wrap prosciutto slice around cheese slice and place in veal roll and stick with
toothpicks. Sprinkle with salt and pepper and dredge threw cannaflour. Brown in skillet on all sides in budder and oil. Remove
and keep warm. Add veal and cover. Simmer 5 minutes. Serve!

Rasta's Pasta

(Also delicious when adding chicken or shrimp)

Ingredients:

1 Box Penne Noodles (or your preference)
1/4 cup Budder
1 Cup Baby Spinach
1 Cup Baby Mushrooms
1 Cup Baby Grape Tomatoes
1 Cup Roasted Red Peppers
2 Cloves Garlic (Chopped)
2 Cups Half and Half
1 Cup Grated Parmesan Cheese
Salt and pepper to taste

OPTIONAL: 1lb Already Cooked Chicken or Shrimp

DIRECTIONS :

First, In a separate pot, boil the penne noodles. Clean and dice spinach, mushrooms, and peppers. Then, in a large skillet pour medicated olive oil over heat, add garlic and saute'.

(OPTIONAL: Clean and cut chicken into strips. Add chicken and saute' until chicken appears cooked on one side. Prepare shrimp. Add shrimp until shrimp appear cooked on one side. Then flip chicken over,

Add spinach, mushrooms, lemon, cannabis oil, and half (8FL oz) the juices and roasted red peppers from the jar in skillet. Saute, stirring occasionally, until all contents in skillet are fully cooked. Drain boiled water from noodles return to pot. Pour entire contents of skillet over the cooked pasta. Enjoy!

Pot Chocolate

INGREDIENTS:

2 Cups of Mary Milk
2 Tsp Budder
4 Tbsp Hot Chocolate Mix
1/4 Cup Chocolate Chips
Chocolate Syrup

Cooking Time: 30min

DIRECTIONS :

First, Grab your pot or saucepan. Pour in mary milk and bud-der, bring to a boil. Once boiling turn down to a simmer. Stir for 20-30 minutes on a simmer. Next, stir in hot chocolate mix and chocolate chips.

Stir until melted. Pour chocolate syrup into bottom of a drink-ing mug. Pour your hot chocolate cannabis concoction into your mug and enjoy! This Chef adds a pirouline waffer in with one big marshmallow for extra happiness!

Canna Cookies Iced Coffee

YOU WILL NEED :

Coffee Maker
Ice Trays (I prefer silicone)
Pitcher
Ziplock Bag
Rolling Pin (or meat mallet)

INGREDIENTS:

Mary Milk
Oreos (vegan friendly)
Coffee

DIRECTIONS :

First, the night before, pour your Mary Milk into a large pitcher. then, take the oreo cookies and put into a large ziplock bag. Grab a rolling pin. Proceed to crumble & smash oreos into tiny pieces. When you feel like your cookies are crumbled enough add them to your pitcher of Mary Milk. Pour your medicated cookies and cream into large ice trays. Freeze until solid.

Brew your fave coffee. Fill drinking glass with your cookies cubes and pour fresh hot coffee over them. Stir it up and start your day.

Sugar & Spiked Rum

Happy Servings: 12 drinks

INGREDIENTS:

1 stick of unsalted infused CANNA BUDDER
2 cups brown sugar
1 tsp cinnamon
1/2 tsp nutmeg
pinch ground cloves
pinch salt
spiced rum (your preference)
hot apple cider

DIRECTIONS:

Soften budder and whip with brown sugar, cinnamon, nutmeg, cloves and salt. Refrigerate until almost firm. Spoon about 2 tablespoons of budder mixture into desired drinking glass/mug.

Top with 2oz spiced rum (your preference) , then fill to top with hot apple cider. Stir and serve immediately.

**For dressing your dish, a sliced apple slice on a cinnamon sugared rim is dee-lish!

Delicious Ending to Any Day! (:

- Catch Deliciously Dee making this recipe paired with her "Dee's Bacon Weaved Grilled Cheese" on Snoop Dogg's MERRYJANE - episode "Smoke in the Kitchen".

https://www.youtube.com/watch?v=tYEd4Jnzi8I

www.MerryJane.com

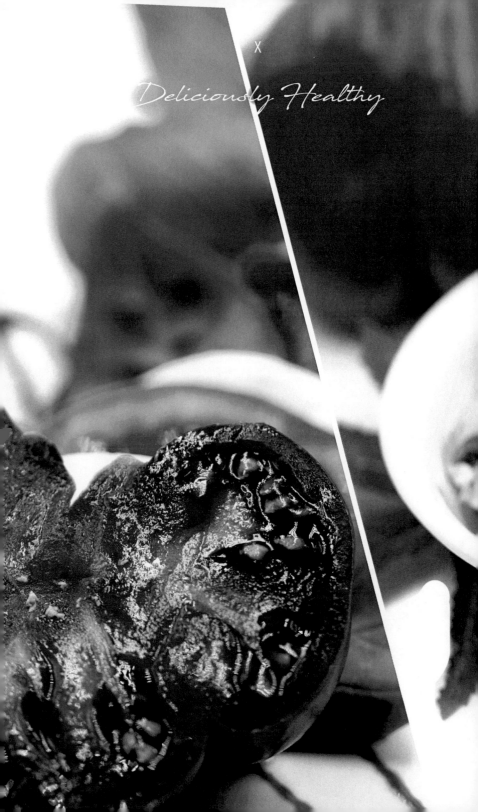

X

Deliciously Healthy

A collection of infused dishes,
for those who enjoy a healthier taste pallet.

Dr. Greenthumb Guac

INGREDIENTS :

4 avocados (peeled, pitted, & mashed)
2 limes (juiced)
2 med tomates
2 onions
1 fresh seeded jalapeño pepper
4 sprigs cilantro (chopped)
1 tsp garlic minced
2 green onions (chopped)
2 tbsp cannabis infused olive oil
salt and pepper to taste

DIRECTIONS :

First, put all ingredients into medium bowl. Mix and Mash all ingredients thoroughly. Place in fridge for 1 to 2 hours.

Serve! Dee-licious! (:

Mary's Mango Salsa

INGREDIENTS :

2 mangos (peeled, seeded, and chopped)
1 (8 oz can) pineapple (drained)
1/4 cup fresh cilantro (chopped)
2 tbsp ginger (peeled, chopped)
1/2 cup red onion (chopped)
1/4 cup rice vinegar
crushed red pepper flakes to taste
1/4 cup cannabis infused olive oil

DIRECTIONS :

Combine mango, pineapple, cilantro, red onion, ginger, vinegar, cannabis oil, and red pepper flakes in a bowl. Mix lightly. Get Happy!

**I serve this with Organic Red Hot Blue Chips...This recipie includes mangos which share a common terpenoid with cannabis known as Myrcene.

Fun Fact: About Myrcene

From what we've learned in my previous articles, it has been made clear that when selecting a strain - look towards the terpenes profiles. This next terpene is viewed as an effective analgesic, anti-bacterial, anti-diabetic, anti-inflamma-tory, anti-insomniatic, anti-proliferative, antipsychotic, and anti-spasmodic.

Myrcene is a monoterpene, the smallest of the terpenes, and is found in very high concentrations in sweet basil, mangoes, hops, and cannabis. Hops and cannabis are in fact cousins, both members of the family Cannabaceae. Myrcene name originates from Myrcia sphaerocarpa, a medicinal shrub from Brazil that contains very high amounts of myrcene which has been used there as a folk remedy for diabetes, diarrhea, dysentery, and hypertension for ages.

While possessing earthly, fruity, cloves-like aromas, myrcene has been shown to change the permeability of cell membrane to allow more absorption of cannabinoids by the brain. Myrcene is pivotal in the formation of other ter-penes and it synergies the antibiotic potential of other terpenes. Conducted in Switzerland, a 1997 study analyzed various cannabis strains for 16 terpenes and found myrcene to be the most abundant terpene out of those studied. For some strains, the myrcene profile can be over half the total content. Other found abundant terpenes include Pinene, Limonene, Linalool, Carene, Humu-lene, Bergamotene, Terpinolene, and Caryophyllene.
Myrcene :

Formula : C10H18 O
Molecular Mass : 136.23404 g/mol
Decarboxylation Point : 115-145 °C(239 °F to 293 °F)
Boiling Point : 168 °C (334 °F)
Vapor Pressure : 7.00 mmHg (20 °C)
Lethal Dose (LD50) : >5g/kg (Compare to Nicotine for mice - 50 mg/kg, for humans - 0.5-1 mg/kg)

Vapor Pressure : 7.00 mmHg (20 °C)
Lethal Dose (LD50) : >5g/kg (Compare to Nicotine for mice - 50 mg/kg, for humans - 0.5-1 mg/kg)

Aroma : Musky, cloves, earthy, herbal with hints of citrus and tropical fruits

Effects : Sedation, relaxation

Medical Value : Antioxidant, Anti-Carcinogenic, Anti-Inflammatory, Anti-Depressant; good for muscle tension, sleeplessness, and chronic pain.

Also Found In : Mango, lemongrass, cloves, thyme, hops

Known Strains High in Myrcene : Pure Kush, El Nino, Himalayan Gold, Skunk #1, White Widow, Grand Daddy Purple GDP

Other Known Factoids : The effects of myrcene has been studied since the 1970s and around the year 2010 a rumor spawned that eating a ripe mango before smoking cannabis would increase the effects or "get you higher." Recent information published by Steep Hill Labs, a well-known medical marijuana testing laboratory located in the Bay Area of California, "most people eating a fresh mango 45 minutes before inhaling cannabis will increase the effects of that cannabis." The man behind this study, Rev. Dr. Kymron de Cesare of Steep Hill, is an advocate of what he has named the "overlapping synergies" between myrcene and other terpenes with various cannabinoids, one of them being how myrcene makes THC more effective.

! KEEP OUT OF REACH OF CHILDREN !
! FOR USE ONLY BY ADULTS 21 YEARS OF AGE OR OLDER !

** IMPORTANT NOTE : Each batch is subject to variable growing conditions, meaning NOT every batch of any given strain will have high levels of these terpenes. The only way to be certain is through a lab's terpene analysis found on label of patients prescription.

Therapeutic attributes of Myrcene :
Analgesic - Relieves pain.

Anti-Bacterial - Slows bacterial growth.

Anti-Diabetic - Helps mitigate the effects of diabetes.

Anti-Inflammatory - Reduces inflammation systemically.

Anti- Insomnia - Helps with sleep.

Anti-Proliferative/Anti-Mutagenic - Inhibits cell mutation- including cancer cells.

Antipsychotic - Tranquilizing effects relieve symptoms of psychosis.

Antispasmodic - Suppresses muscle spasms.

Commonly found in higher concentrations in strains:

Pure Kush

El Nino

Himalayan Gold

Skunk #1

White Widow

Grand Daddy Purple GDP

Summary Of Case Studies Done On Myrcene

Studies :

- The University of Jordan , located in Amman, Jordan, was the research university to investigate Myrcene as the "folk remedy" known cure for diabetes. This 2007 pilot study done on mice convincingly showed that myrcene and also another terpene, thujone, both had a hand in mitigating the effects of diabetes. Of course, further research is needed to better understand the mechanisms of action.

- Myrcene's analgesic effects have been known since the 1990s when a pair of studies demonstrated the pain-relieving power of this terpene. A study done in 1990 found the analgesic effects of myrcene and its unique ability to stimulate the release of endogenous opiates in the body, allowing for pain reduction without any need of external opiate pills. This 1991 study by Lorenzetti Et Ai showed that myrcene demonstrated strong sedative effects and to be promising enough to become a new class of aspirin-like drugs that used a completely different channel in the body. A later 2002 study re-examined and reinforced myrcene showing it to produce barbiturate-like sedative effects in mice in very high doses. It was also shown that these effects increased if citral, a mixture of other terpenes, was present as well.

- This 1990 study, conducted by Da Sila et Ai, sought out to analyze the neurobehavioral effects of myrcene on mice. Despite having strong analgesic and sedative effects, they found that it had NO impact on reducing anxiety, depression, or psychosis. Actually it was documented in the Journal of Phytomedicine (2002), it was found that at high doses myrcene can actually increase anxiety, rather than reduce it.

- In this 2010 study, The National Toxicology Program found "equivocal evidence that beta-myrcene was carcinogenic." This study prompted The California Environmental Protection Agency's Office of Environmental Health Hazard Assessment (OEHHA) to propose listing beta-myrcene as a cancer causing compound under the Safe Drinking Water and Toxic Enforcement Act of 1986. *Not enough scientific research has been done to list beta-myrcene as potentially carcinogenic.

To learn more about terpenes visit www.DeliciouslyDee.com

Mary's Melody

INGREDIENTS :

Great Using Asparagus, Green Beans, & Squash
2 Lbs Veggies (your preference)
1/4 Cup Cannabis oil (olive oil)
1 Tsp Sugar
1/2 Tsp Salt
1/2 Tsp Ground Pepper

DIRECTIONS:

First, Slice up veggies. Sprinkle olive oil. Broil 10 min -Toss that ish- Combine sugar, salt, pepper and sprinkle over veggies. Return to broil another 10 min. Serve.

The Good Stuffed Zucchini

Preheat Oven to 350F

Prep: 15min

Cook: 35min

Happy: 40min

INGREDIENTS :

1 Large Zucchini
3 Tbsp Budder
1/4 White Onion (Chopped)
1 Clove Garlic (Minced)
3/4 Cup Shredded Mozzarella
3 Tbsp Parmesan Cheese
1/2 Cup Bread Crumbs
1 Tsp Italian Herbs
Salt and Pepper to Liking

DIRECTIONS:

First, cut zucchini in 1/4, scoop out middle. In pan melt 3 Tbsp budder and 1/4 chopped onion and minced garlic until dry. Mix 3/4 cup ricotta cheese and 1/2 shredded mozzarella and 3 Tbsp Parmesan cheese and 1/2 cup bread crumbs and 1 Tsp dry Italian herbs. Salt and pepper to liking.

VA Style Crab Cakes

(Cook till brown)

INGREDIENTS :

1lb Back-fin (Lump) Crab meat
2 Eggs (Brown Eggs) Beaten
1/4 Cup Finely Chopped Onion
1/2 Cup 1/4 Cracker Crumbs (Saltine)
3 Tbsp Mayonnaise
1/4 Cup Finely Ground Cannabis
1 Tbsp Prepared Mustard

Serves: 4
Cooking Time: Till Brown

DIRECTIONS :

Gently mix all ingredients. Shape into cakes and saute' in budder until brown. Serve immediately.

*(Happy Chef Tip: Use brown eggs when making crab-cakes it holds together better
than white eggs.)*

Mushroom Kushetta

Prep: 15min

Cook: 15min

Happy: 30min

INGREDIENTS :

1/2 cup (chopped) baby bella mushrooms
1/2 cup (chopped) shitaki mushrooms
1/2 cup (chopped) roasted red peppers
1/4 cup (chopped) sweet chili peppers
2 tbsp capers
1/4 cup cannabis infused olive oil
1/4 cup (shredded) ricata solata cheese
1/4 cup (chopped) baby spinach
1/4 cup (chopped) fresh parsley
sourdough bread - toasted and sliced

DIRECTIONS :

In large skillet, throw in a lil unmedicated olive oil to coat the bottom of the pan. Throw in your mushrooms, roasted red peppers, chili peppers, and capers. Saute for 10 minutes. Then add baby spinach, fresh parsley, and capers. Saute for about 5 minutes. Remove from heat. Stir in cannabis oil. Mix well. On toasted sourdough bread, spread the mixture in skillet over top the sliced breads and top with ricata solata cheese.

Sauce Vinaigrette

INGREDIENTS :

1 1/4 cup cannabis infused olive oil
1 cup balsamic vinager
1/4 cup honey
1 tsp garlic
salt and pepper

DIRECTIONS :

Combine all ingredients in mason jar. Seal on the lid tight. Shake vigorously. If desired put in a pour spout bottle. Oil and vinegar will separate. Shake well before every use. (:

Life's a Peach

Prep: 10min

Cook: 5min

Happy: 30min

INGREDIENTS :

2 (1 in thick) toasted french bread
3 (large) sliced peaches
2 tbsp cannabis infused olive oil
Olive Oil - (for cooking) not medicated
(4 oz) softened goat cheese
2 tsp fresh thyme
Kosher Salt & Pepper

DIRECTIONS:

Set oven rack about 6 inches from the heat source and preheat ovens boiler. Line baking sheet with aluminum foil. Place toast on prepared baking sheet & drizzle olive oil. Stir goat cheese, thyme, pepper together in bowl until softened enough to spread. Spread cheese mixture on each toast (cover whole piece). Top each toast with 3 peach slices, drizzled remaining olive oil over top each piece. Broil in preheated oven until tops and edges are lightly browned, peaches and cheese warmed through... roughly 3 minutes. Remove from heat. Sprinkle cannabis oil over pieces evenly. Serve! Dee-licious!

Canna Couscous

Prep: 5min

Cook: 25min

Happy: 30min

INGREDIENTS :

2 cups vegetable broth
2 cups pearl couscous
1/4 cup mushrooms (chopped) (your preference)
1/8 cup vegan parmesan (grated)
1/8 cup fresh parsley (chopped)
1 tbsp truffle vinaigrette
2 tbsp cannabis infused olive oil
salt & pepper to taste

DIRECTIONS:

In a pot, bring vegetable broth (or water) to a boil. Stir in couscous and cover. Remove from heat and let sit for 8 minutes. Then fluff grains with a fork and set aside.

In a large bowl, combine couscous with mushrooms, fresh parsley, and vegan parmesan. Add in the truffle vinaigrette and CANNA infused olive oil. Mix well. Season with salt and pepper. Place in fridge. - Serve cold.

Ohhh Myyy

(It's all you can say after the first bite!)

Prep: 5min

Cook: 30min

Happy: 35min

INGREDIENTS :

2 (unpeeled) sweet potatoes
1 tsp kosher salt
1/2 tsp chili powder
1/2 tsp paprika
1/2 tsp crushed red pepper
1/8 cup fresh cilantro (chopped)
2 tbsp cannabis infused olive oil

DIRECTIONS:

Put potatoes in large pot of water and cover. Bring to a boil. Then, reduce heat to medium- low and simmer. Cook covered for 10-12 minutes. Drain and let steam dry for 3 minutes. Let cool and then slice potatoes to your preference. (I prefer wedges) Arrange pieces on baking sheet. Brush all sides with olive oil. (un-infused) Bake in preheated oven at 180° C/350° F until potatoes are brown on all sides. (for-twenty minutes) ;-)

In a separate bowl, combine salt, chili powder, paprika, cilantro, and crushed red pepper.

Remove potatoes from oven. Toss potatoes in CANNA infused oil so they are evenly coated and sprinkle over them with combined seasonings. - Toss and Serve.

*I also recommend doing this as a veggie pasta!

Happy Ratatouille

Prep: 25min   Cook: 60min   Happy: 1hr 15min

INGREDIENTS :

2 cups tomato sauce (organic best)
2 cups chopped tomatoes (small, diced)
1 garlic (whole, chopped)
1 cup basil (shredded)
1/4 cup red onion (chopped)
1/4 cup white onion (chopped)
1/4 cup green onions (chopped)
2 tbsp CANNABIS INFUSED olive oil
1 eggplant (thin eggplant, thin sliced)
1 zucchini (thin sliced)

1 yellow squash (thin sliced)
1 sweet potato (medium sized, thin sliced)
1/3 cup crumbled feta cheese
freshly grated black pepper to taste
olive oil for cooking (cooking spray)

DIRECTIONS

Preheat oven at 375 degrees Fahrenheit. Bring 2 cups of water to a rolling boil. Season with salt. Slice sweet potato, boil for 8 minutes and cool down, slice your cooked sweet potatoes and the rest of the vegetables - zucchini, squash, eggplant, onions, garlic, tomatoes.

Spray a 9" round baking dish with cooking spray. Spread layer of tomato sauce, chopped tomatoes, chopped garlic, red onions, white onions, basil, feta, grated pepper and CANNABIS INFUSED olive oil. Mix well, leaving an even spread.

Layer sliced veggies on top. I also love to do this dish as Remy did, in the Disney movie 'Ratatouille' (one of my favorites), making a spiral stack of the slices of delicious veggies for presentation. I do them eggplant, yellow squash, sweet potato, zucchini - step and repeat. ;-D

Cover and bake for 50-60 minutes or until the vegetables are tender. *Tomato sauce will be bubbling !

Let this Deliciously Dosed Dish cool for 5 minutes. Serve with a side of Toasted Garlic French Bread.:

Dragon Fruit Salad

Prep: 15min

Cook: 0min

Happy:20min

INGREDIENTS :

1 dragon fruit (medium size, either white or purple)
1 mango (medium size)
1 blackberries
1 blueberries
1 lemon
2 tablespoons CANNABIS INFUSED coconut oil
fresh cilantro (chopped)

DIRECTIONS

Grab your cutting board and start slicing the dragon fruit and mango. Peel the leaves back from the top of the dragon fruit to peel the skin off, then begin slicing into cubes along with the mango.

Add sliced dragon fruit and mango in large mixing bowl. Add blackberries, blueberries, chopped cilantro, and CANNABIS INFUSED coconut oil.

Slice lemon in half, squeeze halves on top of all ingredients in mixing bowl.

Toss all ingredients well.

The Prevention or The Cure

Prep: 1 Hour 20min

Cook: 45min- 1 Hour

Happy: 20 Hour 20min

INGREDIENTS :

3 whole garlic (chopped)
1 white onion (chopped)
1 red onion (chopped)
1 red pepper (chopped)
1 yellow pepper (chopped)
1 orange pepper (chopped)
5 green onion (chopped)
1 ginger root (thinly shaved slices)
2 gallons chicken broth
whole chicken (cleaned)

2 cups basil (chopped)
2 cups carrots (chopped)
1 lb baby potatoes (chopped)
olive oil (cooking)
3 tbsp dee-carb cannabis (finely ground)

DIRECTIONS

In a large stock pot , pour olive oil in bottom and add the chopped garlic, red onions, and white onions, and all chopped peppers. Cook for 10-15 minutes or until onions, peppers and garlic look charred.

Next add in your cleaned whole chicken, chicken broth, ginger, carrots, baby potatoes and basil.

Boil all ingredients for 45 minutes to 1 hour.

Next, pull out cooked chicken and pull off all the meat. Discard remainder of bird in the trash and add the pulled chicken meat back in the pot. Fill rest of pot with water and boil another 15 minutes.

Serve this feel good soup HOT! (:

Blackberry Kush

INGREDIENTS :

1 cup blackberries
1/4 pineapple (peeled)
1 pear (medium)
1 kiwifruit
10 leaves peppermint
1 tbsp cannabis-infused coconut oil

DIRECTIONS :

DO NOT PUT OIL IN JUICER. *Set oil aside*. Put all ingredients in juicer or blender. Mix well and pour ingredients into preferred drinking glass. Add 1 tbsp of infused cannabis oil into glass. MIX WELL and get happy!

Cypress Kale

INGREDIENTS :

4 large kale leaves
2 (medium) apples
1 (large) cucumber
5 sprigs (small) asparagus
1 lemon (peeled)
2 cups baby spinach
1 tbsp cannabis-infused extra virgin olive oil

DIRECTIONS :

DO NOT PUT OIL IN JUICER. *Set oil aside*. Spinach tends to be difficult in some juicers so I suggest using a blender. Blend remainder of ingredients and pour into desired drinking glass. Add 1 tbsp infused olive oil. MIX WELL and get HAPPY!

Just Beet It

INGREDIENTS :

1 beet root
4 carrots (medium)
3 stalks celery (large)
2 apples (medium)
1/2 (large) cucumber -
1/2 thumb ginger root
1 tbsp cannabis-infused extra virgin olive oil

DIRECTIONS :

DO NOT PUT OIL INTO YOUR JUICER. *Place oil aside*. Put remainder of ingredients into juicer or blender. Blend/Mix well. Then pour into desired drinking glass. Add 1 tbsp of infused cannabis olive oil. MIX WELL and get HAPPY!

Happy Hummus

INGREDIENTS :

2 (15oz) Cans of garbanzo beans (drained)
3 Cloves of Garlic (Minced)
1 Cup Finely Chopped Red Peppers
1 Tsp Crushed Red Peppers
1 Cup Tahini
3 Lemons (Squeezed)
1/4 Cup of Cannabis Oil
Salt to Taste

DIRECTIONS

First, Open the can of beans, strain, and mash. Next, mix all ingredients in a bowl until well blended. Then, place in an air tight container and put in fridge for a couple of hours or until cool. Once cooled... Take out and stir (oil separates from mixture). Measure out a serving and add spices (you preference)

Make sure you stir before every snack as oil separates from mixture. Enjoy your happy hummus!

Serve with chips (Your Choice), crackers, veggies, any way you like!

Most think that eating healthy is expensive. I'll be honest...it is. From a girl raised in farm land I have come to realize that growing your own food is growing your own money. Eating healthy is important! Eating healthy lowers disease risks, increases productivity, gives you more energy, and also certain foods are known to aid with different aliments. There are some tips and tricks to spare your checking account in keeping a healthy grocery bill at low cost.

Here are a few ways to eat healthy on a budget!

Before we begin, let's define healthy food.
What is considered Healthy Foods?

- Water. 1 liter per 1000 calories you expend.

- Fruit. Natural sugar and full of vitamins.

- Vegetables. All kinds, especially green fibrous veggies.

- Whole Grain Food: Pasta, Rice, Oats.

- Protein. Needed for strength.

- Fat. (yes there is healthy fat) A balanced intake of Omega 3, 6, 9 - found listed in cooking oil properties relevant fat information table in chapter 4: "Trichomes, Terps, & Temps."

1. Buy in Bulk

For those necessity items (toilet paper, paper towels, soap, etc) It is wise to purchase those in bulk. It will cost you a lil in the beginning, but saves HUGE in the long run. In this day and age you don't even need to be a Costco or Sams Club Member. +Amazon.com is everyones best friend. One can easily go to the store and buy 6 rolls of TP for $4.99, for 6 rolls? How long will that last. Online buying saves time, gas, and dollars. You can buy 80 rolls of 3 ply TP for as low as $42 dollars. Say Whatttttt!! ;-)

At $4.99 for 6 rolls of TP for 78 rolls (13, 6 packs) you would spend $64.87+tax
Some of you may be like "its 20 dollars"...trust it adds up!

2.Water

For those of you who drink soda like it's water. STOP! There is NO substitute for water. Our bodies are made up of about 70% water. I can not stress on the importance of consuming your daily H2O intake. Soda/Pop whatever you call it is loaded with artificial flavoring and massive amounts of sugar. There is nothing healthy about it, so it is best to cut it completely out of your life. Invest in a reusable water bottle and take it with you everywhere. It's healthier and cheaper.

3. Stick to the list.

Make a list of what you need for a solid meal. Go to the grocery store. Stick to the list...and then GET OUT. Do not go grocery shopping hungry or medicated (high). The munchies will take over and you will walk out the proud owner of aisle 4.

4. One Stop Shop.

Time is money. "This grocery store is cheaper for veggies","This grocery store is better price for meats". I understand if you are looking for a particular food that may not be at the normal grocery store you shop at, but how many grocery stores are you going to go to to find the cheapest food? Save your gas and don't spend your entire day collecting all the items on your grocery list. I shop for the majority of my list at the grocery store nearest my house.

5. Coupons.

This one is pretty self explanatory, but is as true as it gets. I find that clipping coupons to be fun and also can get you out of the normal eating habits. Seeing different foods on sale with a coupon allows you to go out of your eating comfort zone and to try new recipes. "Oh look Brats buy 1 get 2 FREE, I can find a nice recipe for that"

6. Buy Generic.

It may not look very attractive on the packaging, but I guarantee it is more attractive to your check book. Brand-name food is always more expensive. You ARE paying for the name. Food is food. Go generic.

7. Canned Tuna.

Tuna contains as much protein as meat, is healthy, and cheap.

8. Eggs.

Eggs are full of vitamins, high in proteins, and low in price. (there are normally coupons that come in your weekly paper delivery).

* Do not believe the cholesterol & eggs myth. Dietary cholesterol is not bound to blood cholesterol.

9. Fatty Meats.

Fatty meats are more tasty than lean meats and better for your wallets. Don't be deterred by the term "fatty". Fat doesn't make you fat, excess calories do.

10. Whey Protein.

The cheapest source of protein. Nothing beats it. Using whey protein as your post workout shake will aid in recovery.

* Alternate Tuna, Eggs, Fatty Meats, Whey, and Chicken for a healthy source of protein intake.

11. Frozen Vegetables.

Frozen vegetables can be bought in bulk at a discount and stored in your freezer. They take less time to prepare and they don't go to waste if not eaten in time.

*If you can afford fresh veggies, DO IT. Fresh is BEST!

12. Fish Oil.

Fish oil contains Omega-3. The benefits of omega-3 consumption are lowered cholesterol levels, reduced inflammation, and decreased body fat. You need to eat fatty fish 3 times a week to get those benefits which can be costly and time consuming. One teaspoon daily of Liquid Fish Oil is all you need.

13. Multivitamin.

Unfortunately the pesticides used on our food lowers the vitamin levels of those fruits and vegetables. You have two ways around that:

1. Buy organic food= Expensive

2. Use a multivitamin. Years supply for less than $20 (remember what I told you about brands when choosing one)

14. Pack a Snack.

Do you ever add up how much money you spend eating out at lunch during your work week. Cost adds up! Start preparing your meals for the day on waking up. It saves you money (a lot of it), lowers the stress of what you are going to eat that day, and getting into a habit of waking up earlier, make your healthy breakfast and while those eggs are cooking, make your lunch for the day.

15. Eat Less.

Even tho this one seems obvious, but the fact is Americans tend to eat way too much. Our portion sizes are gargantuan compared to other countries. If you are overweight, get on a diet, don't wait for "oh after the weekend" or "my new years resolution"..do it NOW, TODAY, in the PRESENT. Your health & bank account will thank you for it.

16. NO JUNK FOOD.

They call it "junk food" because that's what it is, JUNK! STOP BUYING ANYTHING THAT COMES OUT OF A BOX. It is both Unhealthy and Expensive. You may be thinking "actually it's not that expensive". Think longevity as in health implications. I personally blame all of our health problems by what they are doing to our food. We are consuming unnatural substances in our natural bodies.

As I ALWAYS say, "If it's not of this earth, it's not of your worth." - Deliciously Dee

17. Grow Your Own.

This goes back to what I said in the beginning... "Growing your own food is growing your own money." As is growing your own herbs for seasoning and... Growing your own Medicine, Cannabis.

There are many inexpensive techniques to growing your own.

I prefer the AeroGarden and the Mason Jar Herb Garden Technique for my herbs.

*If y'all didn't know I love mason jars. They are great for everything! Container for your cannabis oil or keeping our buds sealed tight and fresh. (:

Decarboxylated Cannabis Oil

(Photo: AeroGarden)

The sizes vary for both AeroGarden models and in my opinion go wonderfully for any kitchen decor.

(Photo above: Mason Jar Herb Garden)

Not to mention they make your kitchen smell OHmazing even when nothing is cooking.

Now to growing your own meds. How much are you spending on your medicine? I tell you what this part will save you A LOT! Check out some Portable Grow Boxes and SAVE NOW and grow your own medicine.

Triple Chambered, Fully Automated, Continual Harvest, Cabinet Harvest Every Month!
Takes your plants from seed to harvest simply & easily w/ next to no maintenance!

(photo above: www.supercloset.com)

Above photo is example of portable grow boxes. Quite large and not suitable for most homes, there are many different sizes, find the size that is best for you.

**Also: It is proven that growing your own plants/herbs is therapeutic and relieves stress. Talk to your plants, they need the carbon monoxide from us and I guarantee you can trust your plants not to share your problems with the world. A private life is a Happy Life.

18. Ask the Guy behind the Glass.

You ever wonder why fresh foods and meats at the grocery prices are lower than other times...it is because of there delivery. Everywhere is different. But a good tip is ask the guys behind the counter.

These guys are the ones to ask. They can tell you what days are the best days to buy produce and meats per there delivery schedule. It is normally weekly.
My "savings day" is Tuesdays.

19. Follow 1-18.

By making what I have listed a routine I guarantee you will save on groceries by half of what you are spending now. PERIOD.

If you found this information helpful, PLEASE SHARE these tips to a friend. In this economy there are many that are having difficult times and need a few tips to help save. Be The Change. (:

Cannabis Terms

You will hear a lot of industry-specific and company-specific terms. Here we have definitions of some of the more common ones.

Cannabinoids – a family of compounds prevalent in cannabis such as THC, CBD, and CBN. While only THC is psychoactive (can affect your mind) all cannabinoids are bioactive (can affect your body) because we have an endocannabinoid system of receptors on our bodies that vary from person to person.

Cannabinoid profile – the quantity and type of cannabinoids in a given plant or strain. determined by gas chromatography (GC) or more reliably by GC combined with mass spectrometry (GC/MS). Nevada requires testing of levels of both cannabinoids and terpenes and the labeling of all products sold with a print out of that profile so that patients and consumers know what they are getting.

Cannabis – The genus of plants known as marijuana. Because GB Sciences is a very science- oriented company we prefer this scientific term although Nevada law uses marijuana. Cannabis has three species: Sativa, Indicia, and Ruderalis with the first two commonly cultivated for human use.

Hemp – as marijuana is slang for cannabis that is psychoactive, hemp is slang for cannabis that has such low THC levels that it will not make someone high (usually <.3%). Hemp is a legal term, not a scientific one.

Nutrients (or "nutes") - Nitrogen, phospherous, and potassium salts added to RO water to feed the plants

Powdery Mildew (PM) - an undesirable mildew that can crop up on the plants. Developing processes that eliminate PM is a contant goal.

Reverse Osmosis (RO) - a process for removing minerals from tap water so that water used as a base for growing plants is mineral-free. RO water is also used for flushing plants before harvest to minimize excess nutrients in the plants.

Terpenes - are another family of compounds in cannabis such as myrcene and limonene. Terpenes give cannabis its strong odor but also have medicinal properties whether act synergistically with cannabinoids or on their own. For example, GB Sciences has filed a patent application for using myrcene to treat a certain heart condition.

Tissue Culture - a scientific innovation to grow plants more consistently and so that they are healthier. Instead of a large cutting from the plant, our propagation lab takes small amounts of tissue knowns as explants to cultivate a plantlet to be transplanted into the grow.

--

Substitutions

1 tablespoon cornstarch = 2 tablespoons flour (for thickening)

1 cup sifted all-purpose flour = 1 cup plus 2 tablespoons sifted cake flour

1 square chocolate (1 ounce) = 3 tablespoons cocoa plus 1 tablespoon butter

1 cup sour milk = 1 cup sweet milk into which 1 tablespoon vinegar or lemon juice has been mixed. 1 cup buttermilk may also be used.

1 cup sweet milk = 1 cup sour milk or buttermilk plus 1/2 teaspoon baking soda

Weights & Measurements

3 teaspoons = 1 tablespoon
2 tablespoons = 1/8 cup
4 tablespoons = 1/4 cup
5 1/3 tablespoons = 1/3 cup
8 tablespoons = 1/2 cup
10 2/3 tablespoons = 2/3 cup
12 tablespoons = 3/4 cups
14 tablespoons = 7/8 cups

16 tablespoons = 1 cup
1 cup = 8 fluid ounces = 1/2 pint
2 cups = 1 pint
4 cups = 1 quart
4 quarts = 1 gallon
8 quarts = 1 peck
4 pecks = 1 bushel
1 liter = 2.1 pints
1 kilogram = 2.2 pounds (lbs)
28.3 grams = 1 ounce (oz)

Cooking Terms

Baste - To moisten with liquid during cooking, using a spoon or bulb baster. Most often for oven, pot roasts and broiled meats or fish.

Bind - To thicken the liquid of a soup, gravy or stew with a starch such as flour or cornstarch, or with egg yolks.

Blanch - To place in boiling water for a given amount of time and then in cold water for the purpose of partially cooking and peeling.

Blend - To combine ingredients of different textures such as butter and sugar - A gentler mixing than beating.

Braise - To sear or brown in fat, then cook slowly covered, with a minimum of liquid, on stove or in oven.

Breading - A coating of flour and or breadcrumbs used on foods that are to be fried. Beaten egg or milk may be used to help coating adhere.

Coat A Spoon - Custards and sauces which contain egg yolk or corn starch must often cook until they are thick enough to leave a coating on a spoon, indicating their degree of doneness.

Fold - To gently combine a lighter mixture such as beaten egg whites with a heavier mixture such as a cream sauce or cake batter. To do this, place heavier mixture over lighter. Cut down the middle of both with a spatula. Draw spatula toward you, turning the mixture over as you do so. Continue on.

Flambé - Heated brandy (or other spirit) is poured over cooked or partially cooked food and is then ignited and allowed to burn off.

Julienne - Food is cut into very thin, long matchstick strips.

Knead - To work dough by pushing it with the heel of your hand, folding it over and repeating until it has reached degree of smoothness indicated in recipe

Marinate - To soak food, usually meat or fish, in a liquid that will add to its flavor or make it more tender.

Roux - A mixture of fat and flour sautéed together and then adding to liquid to thicken it.

Skim - To remove fat from top of soups and stews, or pan gravies after it has risen - A spoon or bulb baster is best for this. Easiest way to do thorough skimming job is to chill liquid until fat solidifies at the top.

How Much & How Many

BUTTER, CHOCOLATE
2 tablespoons butter = 1 ounce
1 stick or 1/4 lb butter = 1/2 cup
1 square chocolate = 1 ounce

CRUMBS
20 saltine crackers = 1 cup fine crumbs

12 graham crackers = 1 cup fine crumbs

22 vanilla wafers = 1 cup fine crumbs
1 slice of bread = 1/2 cup soft crumbs

NOODLES
4 ounces macaroni (1-1 1/4 cups) = 2 1/4 cups cooked
4 ounces noodles (1 1/2-2 cups) = 2 1/4 cups cooked
4 ounces spaghetti (1-1 1/4 cups) = 2 1/2 cups cooked
1 cup uncooked rice (6 1/2-7 ounces) = 3-3 1/2 cups cooked
1 cup precooked rice = 2 cups cooked

FRUITS, VEGETABLES
juice of 1 lemon = 3-4 tablespoons
grated peel of 1 lemon = 1 teaspoon
juice of 1 orange = 6-7 tablespoons
1 medium apple, chopped = 1 cup
1 medium onion, chopped = 1/2 cup
1/4 pound celery (about 2 stalks) chopped = 1 cup

CHEESE, EGGS
1 pound process cheese, shredded = 4 cups

1/4 pound blue cheese crumble = 3/4- 1 cup

1 large egg beaten = 1/4 cup
12-14 egg yolks = 1 cup
8-10 egg whites = 1 cup

NUTS
1 pound walnuts in shell = 2 cups, shelled
1/4 pound chopped walnuts = about 1 cup
1 pound almonds in shell = about 1 cup, shelled

Herbs & Spices to Try

Allspice - pickling, liver pate, gingerbread, holiday baking, pork and ham, pumpkin and squash dishes.

Anise - cakes, cookies, breads.

Basil - Italian dishes, vegetables, meats, stews and soups.

Bay Leaves - grilled fish, marinades, meat stews and soups.

Cardamom - widely used in Indian Curries as well as in Scandinavian Christmas breads and cookies, stewed fruits and grape jelly.

Cayenne Peppers - egg dishes, cream sauces, cheese dishes and spreads.

Chervil - egg dishes, salad dressings, cream sauces, cottage cheese dips.

Chives - fresh or dried are excellent in dips, salads, garnishing for potatoes and soups - steep dried chives in hot water 15 minutes before using.

Cinnamon - toast, tea, cocoa, coffee, fruit desserts and pies, rice pudding, middle eastern meat and rice dishes.

Cloves - ham, apple desserts, spiced tea, tomato bouillon, creamed onions.

Curry Powder - mayonnaise or cream sauces for fish, lamb, poultry.

Dill - cucumber salads, salmon, sauce for boiled beef, chicken or fish.

Garlic - used mostly in French, Italian, Spanish and Chinese recipes, excellent with lamb, shellfish, in salad dressings and appetizer dips. Garlic salt or powder should be used only when fresh garlic is not available.

Ginger - broiled chicken, pot roasts, peach desserts, fish sauces, barbecues, holiday baking.

Marjoram - meat stews and soups, dried beans and peas.

Mint - use fresh or dried mint to flavor sauce for lamb, and fresh sprigs in cold drinks, salads, peas and pea soup and Middle Eastern yogurt sauce.

Nutmeg - rice and sweet puddings, eggnog, spinach, mushrooms, wild rice, cauliflower.

Oregano - meat and poultry roasts and stews, vegetable casseroles, Italian sauces.

Paprika - meat and poultry goulashes, broiled fish, rarebits, decorative topping.

Rosemary - lamb, veal, poultry.

Saffron - risotto, pilaf, paella, Swedish coffee cake, bouillabaisse.

Sage - pork, poultry or onion stuffings, sausage meat.

Savory - string beans, cabbage, salad dressings, dried peas and beans.

Tarragon - green mayonnaise for fish, béarnaise sauce, roasted poultry,salads and dressings.

Thyme - clam chowder, meat and vegetable soups and stews, egg dishes.

Americans For Safe Access Cannabis Advocacy Group
http://safeaccessnow.org

NORML Advocacy Group for Legislative Policy Reform
http://www.norml.org

DigiPath Labs
http://www.digipathlabs.com

GBSciences Medical Cannabis Research Company
https://www.gbsciences.com

https://en.wikipedia.org/wiki/Terpenoid
https://www.verywell.com/types-of-marijuana-22323

Penalties Nevada -
http://norml.org/laws/item/nevada-penalties-2

Consuming concentrates
:https://www.coloradopotguide.com/colorado-marijua-
na-blog/2015/may/10/how-to-consume-marijuana-concen-
trates/

Wagner H, Ulrich-Merzenich G. (2009) Synergy Research:
Approaching a new generation of phytopharmaceuticals.
Phytomed. 16:97-110.

Howlett AC et al. (2002), International Union of Pharmacology, XXVII. Classification of cannabinoid receptors. Pharmacol. Rev. 54:161-202.

Klingeren BV & Ham MT (1976) Antibacterial activity of
delta-9-tetrahydrocannabinol and cannabinol. Antonie van
Leeuwenhoek 42:9-12.

Ramen A et al. (1995) Antimicrobial effects of tea-tree oil and its major components on Staphlococcus aureus, 5 epidermidis. Lett Appl Microbiol 21(4):242-5.

Malfait AM et al. (2000) The nonpsychoactive cannabis constituent cannabidiol is an oral anti-arthritic therapeutic in murine collagen-induced arthritis. Proc Natl Acad Sci USA 97:9561-6.

Turner et al. (1980) Constituents of cannabis sativa L. XVII. A review of the natural constituents. J Nat Prod 43:169-304.

Hammerschmidt etal. (1993) Chemical composition and antimicrobial activity of essential oils of Jasonia candicans and J. Montana. Planta Med 59(1):68-70.

Langenheim JH (1994) Higher plant terpinoids: a phytocentric overdue of their ecological roles. J. Chem. Ecol. 20:1223-1279.

Offord et al. (1997) Mechanism involved in the chemoprotective effects of rosemary extract studied in human liver and bronchial cells. Cancer Lett 114:275-81.

Gerritsen et al. (1995) Flavonoids inhibit cytokine-induced endothelial cell adhersion protein gene expression. Am J Path 147:278-92.

Russo et al. (2000) Pharmacology of the essential oil of hemp at 5-HT receptors. Poster at 41 Annual mtg of the Amer Soc of Pharmacognosy July 22-26, Seattle WA.

Berenbaum MC (1989) What is synergy? Pharmacol Rev. 41:93-141.

McPartland JM & Russo EB (2001) Cannabis and cannabis extracts: greater than the sum of their parts? The Haworth Prss, Inc. pp. 103-132.

Science - How Stuff Works -
http://science.howstuffworks.com/marijuana3.htm
http://headsup.scholastic.com/students/the-science-of-marijuana

Getting Legal - GettingLegal.com

Scientific white sheets written by Dr. Andrea Small-Howard of GBSciences Medical Cannabis Research Facility. http://www.gbsciences.com

Drug Facts -
https://www.drugfacts.com/marijuana

Wikipedia Sources:

https://en.wikipedia.org/wiki/Trichome , https://en.wikipedia.org/wiki/Smoke_point , https:/en.wikipedia.org/wiki/cannabidol

PubChem - Chemistry Boiling Points of different cannabinoids, terpenoids, flavonoids :
http://www.pubchem.com

Cannabis-Med
:http://www.cannabis-med.org/data/pdf/2001-03-04-7.pdf

NORML : http://www.canorml.org/healthfacts/vaporizer-studfy1.html

Terpene Profiling : http://thewercshop.com/services/terpene-profiling-services/

Diet Nutritional Reference :
https://www.jonbarron.org/diet-and-nutrition/healthiest-cooking-oil-chart-smoke-points

Learn about Marijuana : http://learnaboutmarijuanawa.org/

factsheets/cannabinoids.htm

Dr. Grinspoon "therapeutic essemble" - http://hightimes.com/culture/the-ensemble-effect-not-the-entourage-effect-says-dr-grinspoon/

Truth On Pot : www.truthonpot.com (photo of history of cannabis)

Facts about Myrcene: www.pubchem.com, www.pubmed.com, www.theleafonline.com
https://www.leafly.com/news/cannabis-101/terpenes-the-flavors-of-cannabis-aromatherapy
https://www.spectrumchemical.com/MSDS/M0070.PDF
https://en.wikipedia.org/wiki/Myrcene
http://www.internationalhempassociation.org/jiha/jiha4208.html
http://steephill.com/science/terpenes
https://unitedpatientsgroup.com/blog/2012/04/11/terpene-and-cannabis-by-rev-dr-kymron-de-cesare-of-halent-laboratories
http://theleafonline.com/c/science/2014/09/terpene-profile-myrcene/
https://www.ncbi.nlm.nih.gov/pubmed/1753786
https://www.ncbi.nlm.nih.gov/pubmed/1983154
https://www.ncbi.nlm.nih.gov/pmc/articles/PMC2503660/
https://www.ncbi.nlm.nih.gov/pubmed/12587690
https://www.ncbi.nlm.nih.gov/pubmed/1753786
https://www.ncbi.nlm.nih.gov/pubmed/1797273
https://www.ncbi.nlm.nih.gov/pubmed/12587690
https://oehha.ca.gov/proposition-65/crnr/notice-intent-list-beta-myrcene
https://en.wikipedia.org/wiki/Terpenoid

Deliciously Dee - The Happy Chef Cookbook: Food Prepared Plated & Photographed by: Kayley Thomas-Garrett @KayleyDaily www.kayleylizdigital.com Book Design and Layout by: Kayley Thomas Garrett. Other Photography by Logan Pochatko, JovaFilms, Digipath Labs, DNA Genetics @flyhighclub, Shawn Gower of Moxie Colorado, Fotogasm, Karen Russell, Web sourced here)

Music Promo by Hip-Hop artist and cannabis activist B-Real of Cypress Hill "The Prescription" as Free Download after purchase

Thank you to BREAL.TV , MERRYJANE.com , Warner Bros. Cooking on High, Semmelboomboom Productions/DeliciouslyDee - This Taste Funny, DigiPath Labs Las Vegas, and GBSciences Cultivations Labs and Chief Scientist Dr. Andrea Small-Howard.

About the Author

Meet Deliciously Dee,

Birth name Danielle Russell, friends and colleagues call her Dee. Dee has been making edibles or medicinal edibles with cannabis from 2006 to present. In 2014 she published the first edition of this cannabis cookbook including hip-hop album "The Prescription" from hip-hop artist and MMJ patient B-Real of Cypress Hill. The year 2015 was the year of legalization for medical marijuana for the state of Nevada. Dee was the first licensed MMJ Production Kitchen in the state of Nevada located in the fabulous city of Las Vegas.

Beginning of 2016, Dee partnered with GB Sciences Inc., a Medical Cannabis Research Company. In October 2016, GB Sciences filed patent applications for the Treatment of Chronic Arthritis, Crohn's Disease, Inflammatory Bowel Disease, and Asthma; Proprietary Cannabinoid-Containing Complex Mixtures for Treatment of Inflammatory Disorders.

Dee currently owns and operates her own MMJ Production Extraction Lab, and Kitchen partnered with GB Sciences - Cultivation

Labs™ in Las Vegas, Nevada. Her company's edible line, Relax With Happy ™, are hand-crafted, single doses, designed to take the edge off your day. Look for Relax With Happy™ Edibles at your local dispensary.

Relax With Happy

Medicinal Chews

Cake Bites

Ambers

To know more about Deliciously Dee™ visit her blog at:
www.DeliciouslyDee.com

Also make sure to check out her YouTube channel:

Deliciously Dee
https://www.youtube.com/deliciouslydee

For How To recipe videos on her show called:

Deliciously Dee's - THE HAPPY CHEF

and for a REAL inside to the science behind the
cannabis plant in:

Deliciously Dee's - GREEN SCIENCE

Follow us @edibledee & @relaxwithhappy on social medias:

INSTAGRAM

https://www.instagram.com/edibledee

https://www.instagram.com/relaxwithhappy

TWITTER

https://www.twitter.com/edibledee

https://www.twitter.com/relaxwithhappy

FACEBOOK

https://www.facebook.com/edibledee/

https://www.facebook.com/relaxwithhappy/

BLOG, WEBSITE, MERCHANDISE

www.DeliciouslyDee.com

Thank You!

This is my high chart and here I'd like to reach out a special thank you to all my guinea pigs over the years. Glad to have medicated you all and enjoy to all those who have purchased my book.

Happy Medicating!

Louis F., Lenny D, Eitan M., Dory N., Courtney B., Marshall B., Lynnie R., Stephen M., Angie M., Richard O., Joseph R., Karen R., Jason L., Julie W., Tim B., Maddy B., Jamie C., Lindsay C., Tiffany C., Melissa L., Baxter S., Brett C., Slim K., Joey H., Chris F., Chris E., Chris El., Chris J., Louis L., Bobby W., Barret G., Ashely E., Parker E., Bill G., Keith P., Mike B., Milo B., Christina M., Kenny M., Erin B., Smith C., Denny T., Gary R., Victoria P., Brian J., Thomas E., Carrie K., Kyles S., Pyne G., Dave S., Eddie C., Michael L., Chad D., Everette P., Jamie D., Tiffany C., Brian F., Erinn M., Bryce L., Alleigh M., Jessa E., Trey F., Clay R., Miguel M., Shidia L., Nick M., Andrus K., Chris B., Karen I., Ashley B., Ct C., Brandon B., Oscar C., Heather S., Rachel S., Britney B., Katheryne B., Chad L., Robert B., Thomas I., Lula T., Josh B., Alyssa B., Edward T., Brandon B., Timmy C., Gus C., Manda S., Samantha R., Kevin B., Matt M., Aaron S., Andrew G., Brian P., Danielle H., William H., Jamie Rae M., Erin R., Colby B., Bryant M., Duana S., Tim A., Luis M., Nick R., Melissa R., Joe C., Miles F., HarryR., Stanley H., Anthony H., StevenH., Faheem N., Ned S., Ossama S., Thomas I., Nathan S., Marc F., George C., Benzel B., Zakir K., Denise D., Kayley T., David S., Andrea S. , Aaron S., Kevin C., Josh W., Sailene O., Rachel T., Chris C., Noelle S., John P., Monica P., John D., Mike L., Shane T., Tom A., Michael L., Joe N., Brian F., Rebecca S., Greg C., Shelby S., Todd D., Craig E., Kenji F., Dina B., Jason B., Josh B., Bradie J., Chris E., Michael P., Steve A., Steven C., Chris S., Eric P., Shawn G., Michelle R., Steve D., John E., Kyle B., Julian H., Marshall M., Clifford S., Reggie N., Melissa E., Dana R., Pharrel W., Chad H., Britney

D., Brandi S., Meli, Alaina S., Krista R., Gerald G., Diamante B., Larsa P., Tommy C., Maricela C., Elle N., X, Liv T., Andrea S., Chris H., Tasha, Ksenia, Reyna, Garrett, Justice, Kevin K., Sam T., Butch B., Skillz H., Joe R., Anthony B., Ulrich R., Craig E., Brian M., Meredith S., Barley K., And any others i may have left out!

Recipe Notes

Thank you for reading! Happy Medicating!

The Happy Chef
Deliciously Dee